ALL THESE

LONDON : HUMPHREY MILFORD

OXFORD UNIVERSITY PRESS

ALL THESE

BY

PAUL REVERE FROTHINGHAM

CAMBRIDGE, MASSACHUSETTS
HARVARD UNIVERSITY PRESS
MCMXXVII

COPYRIGHT, 1927
BY THE PRESIDENT AND FELLOWS OF HARVARD COLLEGE

PRINTED IN THE UNITED STATES OF AMERICA

"All these were honored in their generation and were the glory of their times."
ECCLESIASTICUS, XLIV, 7.

"No man is truly great who is great only in his life time. The test of greatness is the page of history."
HAZLITT.

CONTENTS

Introduction.	By *M. A. DeWolfe Howe*	ix
Memoir.	By *Robert Grant*	3
I.	John Cotton	17
II.	John Fiske again	45
III.	John Ruskin	73
IV.	The Historian as Preacher	105
V.	The Mysticism of Maeterlinck	139
VI.	By Way of Contrast	171
VII.	Edward Everett Hale	191
VIII.	William Everett	213
IX.	George Hodges	255
X.	Cromwell's Head	273
XI.	A Great Character: Charles W. Eliot	291

INTRODUCTION

THE title of this volume, "All These," was of the author's own choosing. In the weeks before his sudden and untimely death, on November 27, 1926, he appears to have assembled his biographical essays with a view to their publication as a book. Though I was constantly meeting him at that time in the Boston Athenæum, our common working-place, he never spoke to me of these papers or of his intention with regard to them. It was not until several weeks after his death that his widow asked me if I would examine them, and, in the event of considering their publication as a book desirable, undertake the supervision of that process on her behalf.

The pleasure I found in reading the little collection seemed to me one in which many would welcome an opportunity to share. The book, I felt, would justify itself abundantly both as a contribution to biographical literature and as a memorial of a citizen, a minister of the Christian religion, a man of letters, and a friend, singularly admired and beloved in all these relationships. There has seemed, moreover, a special fitness in the production of the book under the auspices of the Harvard University Press. As a graduate of Harvard College and the Harvard Divinity School, as an official of the University for many years, through his membership in the Board of Overseers and the Board of Preachers, he was so truly and completely a son of Harvard that the seal of the University on this the last of his books is a symbol of which the significance needs merely to be suggested.

There is a further significance in the title "All These." It is a symbol of the comprehensiveness of the sympathies which made Paul Frothingham precisely what he was. The subjects of the ensuing papers — written chiefly for local audiences, including his parishioners in the Arlington Street Church in Boston, for the *Harvard Theological Review*, for the Massachusetts Historical Society — are widely various. Yet with them all he possessed and felt a definite kinship. With John Cotton, an ancestor, and with William Everett, a cousin, there was the actual kinship of blood. With other

INTRODUCTION

men of thought and action, Froude, Ruskin and Fiske, Cromwell and President Eliot, there was a close kinship of the spirit. It is told that his uncle, Octavius Brooks Frothingham, the brilliant expositor of a new religious philosophy, once said, "I have spent my life tearing down; Paul is building up." The constructive, inclusive temper of his mind, which carried his sympathies and his influence so far beyond the bounds of a single religious body, were those that prepared him for a generous acceptance of the principles underlying the League of Nations, and made him its steadfast and eloquent advocate among his fellow countrymen. If this book, taking form when his labors were brought to their abrupt end, contains no pages bearing directly upon the chief public interest of his later years, — the League and its progress, — the sympathies which it reveals speak in their very quality for a heart and head that caused him to stand where he stood, all unequivocally, with respect to the world-wide organization of human society. He was the friend of human beings, near and far, the clear exemplar, in all his contacts, of the vitalizing power of a spiritual relation with life in every manifestation, whether of the temporal or of the unseen. To bear any part in the fulfillment of a plan — the publication of this book — which was occupying his mind as his life neared its end, is indeed a privilege.

So much for the book now offered to the public — for its own sake and as a memorial to Paul Revere Frothingham. For the circumstances of the life out of which it grew its readers may inform themselves, or refresh their memories, by means of a memoir prepared by Frothingham's lifelong friend, Judge Robert Grant, for the Massachusetts Historical Society, and included, with some abridgment, in this volume through the great kindness of its author and that Society.

M. A. DeWolfe Howe

Boston, June, 1927.

MEMOIR

MEMOIR

PAUL REVERE FROTHINGHAM, a distinguished and much-loved preacher of the Unitarian faith, a patriotic citizen, and a member of the Massachusetts Historical Society since March 15, 1915, had theologians among his ancestors in both the male and female lines. His father, Thomas Bumstead Frothingham (1819–1880), himself a merchant, was a son of Nathaniel Langdon Frothingham, D.D. (1793–1870), Harvard College, 1811, Minister of the First Church of Boston (Unitarian) from 1815 to 1850; and an uncle was Rev. Octavius Brooks Frothingham (1822–1895), Harvard College, 1843, with whom he had a close and sympathetic friendship. His mother, Anna Parsons Lunt (1830–1896), was a daughter of William Parsons Lunt, D.D. (1805–1857), Harvard College, 1823, for many years minister of the Church of the Presidents in Quincy.

[His grandfather Lunt, and, in lesser degree, his grandfather Frothingham, as it appears from the full text of Judge Grant's memoir, belonged to the conservative wing of the Unitarian movement; his uncle Octavius, somewhat later, to the radical. "Paul Frothingham," writes Dr. Crothers, as quoted in the memoir, "began where his uncle left off. He took liberty for granted. The battle for free thought was, so far as he was concerned, fought and won. To organize spiritual freedom and to make it effective in the lives of ordinary men and women was the difficult task to which he gave himself." Judge Grant proceeds:]

Paul Frothingham was born July 5, 1864, at Jamaica Plain, Massachusetts. His mother's sister, Lucretia Lunt, had married Paul Joseph Revere, who fell at Gettysburg, "following a brother who the year before had laid down his life at Antietam," and he was named Paul Revere for this maternal uncle by marriage. "A 'real boy,' like the rest of us," so writes his brother Langdon, "joining heartily in all our games, perfectly at home in the water and on it, a splendid skipper of the Cape catboat, who sailed many a race in the early days of the Beverly Yacht Club on Buzzard's Bay." His education began at Mrs. Walker's private school, Jamaica Plain, the Boston Latin School, and Stone's private school, from which he entered Harvard in the class of 1886. He graduated from the College *cum laude*. He was a pole vaulter on the track team.

He immediately entered the Harvard Divinity School, from which he received the S.T.B. degree in 1889, and also from the College in the same year the degree of A.M. But in the summers of 1887 and 1888 he was already preaching at the Unitarian Chapel at Tiverton, Rhode Island. In October, 1889, at the age of twenty-five, he was appointed an assistant to Rev. William J. Potter, Minister of the First Congregational Society (Unitarian), New Bedford, whom later he succeeded. Here he remained until 1900, declining calls to pastorates both in Chicago and in Washington. On June 14, 1892, he was married to Miss Anna Clapp of Pittsfield and New York. Glowing reports of his ability as a preacher and of the affection and esteem felt for him by his parishioners in New Bedford led to an invitation in 1900, which he decided to accept, to become the minister of the Arlington Street Church, Boston, in succession to Rev. John Cuckson. This "Church in Dr. Channing's day was known as the Federal Street Church, and it had been founded in Boston in 1730 by Scotch Presbyterians. A barn at what is now Federal and Franklin Streets, later remodelled and enlarged, served as a meeting place until a new meetinghouse was built in 1774. In this the Massachusetts delegates met and accepted the Federal Constitution in 1788. A third meetinghouse served the congregation from 1809 to 1859. In the vestry of this meetinghouse the American Unitarian Association was founded in 1825. The Church then moved to Arlington Street and the present meetinghouse was dedicated in 1860. It is one of the noblest types of the style made famous by the London churches of Sir Christopher Wren and his successors." The ministers in succession to Dr. Channing had been Ezra Stiles Gannett, 1824–1871; John F. W. Ware, 1872–1881; Brooke Herford, 1882–1892; John Cuckson, 1892–1900, under all of whom and including Paul Revere Frothingham, 1900–1925, the writer of this memoir has sat with tolerable assiduity from boyhood to old age, except for a few years of deviation during a part of Dr. Cuckson's term of service.

The quarter of a century, plus a single year, — for he died suddenly on November 27, 1926, while still apparently vigorous in every respect, — which covered Dr. Frothingham's ministry at the Arlington Street Church was the period when he became publicly known as a fearless but fundamentally reasonable and sympathetic interpreter of Unitarian doctrine. But doctrine in his sermons was always secondary to a desire to aid his listeners to find their way through the jungle of impediments which turn modern men and women away from goodness. Spirituality to him meant first of all right decision on the daily issues which confront an intelligent community seeking to do God's will, and, though rarely, if ever, dogmatic, he never hesitated to point out those issues and to indicate the fallacious choice. Yet the most potent effect of his earnestness even when he felt most intensely was his never-failing wish to understand and willingness to tolerate another's point of view. This was true both of daily personal contact and his attitude toward other communions. As Dr. George A. Gordon eloquently said of him on the twenty-fifth anniversary of his installation at Arlington Street Church: "Dr. Frothingham is two things of great value in the higher life of this city. He is a man with a distinctive and decided view of the Christian religion and of the world's most urgent need. He is at the same time able and willing to transcend his inherited and personal point of view, and to stand in the fellowship of all who worship God, and serve mankind. *He stands on the bridge of his own great liner, and at the same time looks upon the liners plowing through the same seas, towards the same or similar goals, and salutes them, bidding them Godspeed.*" (Italics mine.)

Paul Frothingham, by his human quality, endeared himself to his parishioners and to all with whom he was closely associated. He exhaled none of the aroma of the pronounced cleric, but met both the redeemed and the unredeemed alike upon a footing of everyday manly good fellowship which took to itself neither pretension nor ceremony. No one was more alive to what was going on in mundane affairs than he, and none more appreciative of genial clean mirth and agreeable companionship. He was wholly free from self-importance and was warmly appreciative of the talents or virtues of his friends. His convictions, though never obtruded, could not be trifled with or trampled on, however. I might have forgotten having said to him one day in defence of a "pretty good world" that preferred to be let alone, "I wish that I might never hear the word reform uttered again," had I not been rebuked, though not by name, in next Sunday morning's sermon. To him my impetuous ebullition seemed sacrilege, for nothing was dearer to both his heart and conscience than the hope of a constantly improving world and dwellers therein moved to make it better. It is significant that the text for his twenty-fifth anniversary sermon was "And these all, having obtained a good report through faith, received not the promise; God having provided some better thing for us, that they without us should not be made perfect" (Hebrews xi, 39, 40); and he elucidated the paradox by saying: "And yet, there is no mistake about this utterance. The unknown author of the famous faith chapter in the Epistle to the Hebrews meant precisely what he said. And he said that while you, and I, and all of us, are helped, and shaped, and guided, by the great and good of former ages whom we remember and rejoice to praise, it is also true that those same saints, reformers and upbuilders are dependent upon us to make them, by our actions, whether more and more perfect, or of less and less account."

It is easy to understand, therefore, that he was not content with the four walls of any tabernacle. His zeal for righteousness constantly sought lay and patriotic outlets outside the decorous constraints of the pulpit. All public questions which seemed to involve an ethical principle absorbed him. He chafed, though never with impatience, at our slowness in entering the great war after the sinking of the *Lusitania*, for he recognized from the first that the triumph of German militarism would mean the death of liberty. And after the conflict was over, his love of peace, his never discouraged though constantly disappointed hope that mankind would by means of the League of Nations eventually make war impracticable, and that his country should sit at the Council table, became his foremost practical aim. Dr. Park said truly in his tribute before this Society that "one of the great sorrows of his life was that we were not in the League of Nations." Year after year he visited Geneva in order to acquire knowledge and inspiration by which to overcome the political bias of his countrymen.

He was a member of the Board of Preachers to Harvard University, 1899-1902, 1909, 1910, and continuously since 1914 until his death. He was elected an Overseer of the University, 1904-1910, and again for the term 1918-1924. He took an active part in bringing about the union of the Andover Theological and the Harvard Divinity Schools. Harvard conferred upon him in 1915 the honorary degree of S.T.D. On the occasion of his twenty-fifth anniversary President Lowell said of him: "The cares of a great parish are enough to tax any man's strength, but he has given of himself freely and you have lent him for the service of the University. During one-half of his pastorate here he has been an Overseer, and during more than a half of the time he has been a member of the Board of Preachers. Thousands of young men, not only there but in other colleges, have listened to his powerful sermons and many of them have consulted him in their perplexities."

Dr. Frothingham was also a Trustee of the Perkins Institution for the Blind; President of the Massachusetts Cremation Society; a Fellow of the American Academy of Arts and Sciences; Vice-President of the Greater Boston Federation of Churches; a director of the Associated Charities (now the Family Welfare Society), and a member of various other literary, charitable, and social organizations. As a member of this Society he communicated Memoirs of Dean George Hodges, Edward Everett Hale, and William W. Crapo. He was a frequent attendant at the meetings of the Society, and while preparing his biography of Edward Everett, read several of the chapters before our members. In March, 1923, he addressed the Society on the Assembly of the League of Nations.

His biography of Edward Everett, orator and statesman, appeared in 1925; a labor of love on which he had been engaged for a number of years. A sister of his grandmother Frothingham was Edward Everett's wife; and though William Everett, their son, had always intended to write his father's life, he had failed to do so. To me the Everett biography seems an excellent piece of literary work, lucid and readable, justly eulogistic, and yet impartial. He sets in relief his brilliant subject's talents and public services, without claiming for him the immortality already accorded him while alive. It is edifying to recall what a very eminent man Edward Everett was in his day, and that no American before his time or since has (after preliminary canters as Pastor of the famous Brattle Street Church at nineteen and Professor of the Greek language at Harvard University at twenty-one) held in stately sequence all the offices of Member of Congress, Governor of Massachusetts, Minister at the Court of St. James, President of Harvard College, Secretary of State (in succession to Daniel Webster), and United States Senator. It required a sage and discriminating biographer not to be lured into superlatives by such a tiara of major titles reinforced by rare eloquence. To quote Dr. Crothers again: "There was a certain audacity in his choice of a subject, for Everett after enjoying great fame in his lifetime had become a shadowy figure to this generation. Nevertheless Frothingham succeeded in making him live again. He did this without resorting to the means by which biographers of the new school add brilliancy to their work by ironical touches. A certain old-fashioned stateliness in Everett's manner invites irreverent comment, but Frothingham wisely abstained. He points out fairly enough the limitations of one who was a notable and versatile American and very influential in his day."

Had Frothingham lived longer, his literary tastes would have asserted themselves more prominently. He had already asked to be relieved from a portion of the church routine in order to have more leisure. Although the ardent tributes paid to him at the twenty-fifth anniversary of his installation in the Arlington Street Church gave fresh zest to the vision that here was the ideal site for a Unitarian Cathedral, he allowed those who knew him intimately to gather that the time was not far off when he would seek at least a larger division of labors if not retirement in order to write. This proceeded from no lack of vigor, for to all appearances he was as strong as ever, but from the preference, which was perhaps in the blood, for a wider field for his pen than active service as a pastor afforded. One great merit of his sermons apart from their earnestness and scholarly diction was the clarity of every proposition presented, and perhaps he felt that the fire which glowed within him at all times, but perforce weekly, would have more scope in sustained effort. But be this as it may, his work was already done.

Paul Frothingham was still at his best when he died, on November 27, 1926. Sixty-two years had in no wise dimmed the sparkle of the clear, honest gaze which inspired both affection and confidence, or hardened the firm but genial mouth which told, before he spoke, of intelligent sympathy. Where was there in our community a more spiritually honest man? Where one more zealous for righteousness yet freer from the defects of the fanatic? Where one more simple and essentially human? Deep and abiding as were his convictions, he preferred to be thought of as a pilot of Christian souls through the complexities of modern living rather than as a hard and fast theologian. He was a clergyman — of the kind now more common than formerly — with whom laymen throw off their reserve so as to forget that he is one; and to him Kipling's familiar lines —

E'en as he trod that day to God so walked he from his birth,
In simpleness and gentleness and honour and clean mirth —

apply with all the greater force because he rejoiced in being a Christian minister. He will be remembered as a modern in the best sense, who carried on the tradition of his sect with unswerving fidelity to its tenets, yet whose interest in exact belief was always secondary to zealous promotion of upright living in this world, a world which to him was never narrow and always rich in opportunity.

ROBERT GRANT.

JOHN COTTON

JOHN COTTON [1]

IN 1630, in the spring of that important year, a little group of people was gathered on the deck of a vessel that lay at anchor in Southampton Water. A man in clerical dress is preaching to them, and men and women listen to his telling words in rapt attention. The preacher has taken his text from II Samuel, vii, 10: "Moreover I will appoint a place for my people Israel, and will plant them, that they may dwell in a place of their own, and move no more."

They are well-to-do, these men and women, — many of them people of prominence and some distinction, — and they are evidently emigrants, just setting forth to take possession of some distant land. A stranger might have gathered this from the speaker's words. For, after dwelling on the more scholastic meanings of his text, the preacher gave it application to the things at hand. "Have special care," he said, as he drew his sermon to a close, "have special care that you ever have the ordinances planted amongst you, or else never look for security. As soon as God's ordinances cease,

[1] This Address was delivered at the unveiling of a statue of John Cotton in the First Church, Boston, October 10, 1907.

your security ceaseth likewise; but if God plant his ordinances among you, fear not, he will maintain them." And then he closed his exhortation with these impressive words: "Neglect not walls, and bulwarks, and fortifications for your own defence; but ever let the name of the Lord be your strong tower, and the word of his promise the rock of your refuge. His word that made heaven and earth will not fail, till heaven and earth be no more."

The preacher was John Cotton, one of the most learned and famous clergymen in England at that day, and the men and women were the people of Winthrop's company who were setting out for Massachusetts Bay to become the founders of the town of Boston. Cotton at that time was vicar of St. Botolph's Church in Boston, Lincolnshire, where for eighteen years he had been settled. He had made the journey, however, to Southampton with several of his friends who were among the emigrants, and there, as lately has been learned, he preached the sermon which was afterwards published under the title of "God's Promise to his Plantation." He was the John Robinson of the Boston Pilgrims, and his words deserve a place beside the well-remembered words that were spoken at Delftshaven.

Three years now passed, and behold a very different scene presents itself, again upon a vessel near Southampton — a scene in which the preacher is

JOHN COTTON

once more the central figure. He is now a fugitive from persecution, having escaped with difficulty the searchers whom Archbishop Laud has laid upon his track. The ports of England are all watched with care that the "pestilential Puritan" may be waylaid. Under cover of the night, however, a ship, which was diligently searched when she put in at the Isle of Wight, is "lying to" beneath the high white cliffs which gird and grace the lovely and romantic coast of southern England. A boat is rowed off from the shore, and the half-concealed figure of a man is helped on board the vessel, which quickly bears away and shapes her course across the waters of the wide Atlantic. John Cotton has escaped from his native land to become that "great Cotton," that "Apostle of his age" whom his descendants of the seventh and eighth generations have honored by this monument which to-day we come to dedicate.

John Cotton was perhaps the greatest, probably the most distinguished, and surely the most influential, of all the early Puritan divines who stamped their life and thought upon the destinies of this new world. Professor Tyler, in his history of American literature, has called him "the unmitered Pope of a pope-hating commonwealth," and says that "he wielded with strong and brilliant mastership the fierce theocracy of New England. Laymen and clergymen alike recognized his supremacy and rejoiced in it." He was the friend of Sir Harry Vane, and the counsellor of Cromwell. In the days of the English Commonwealth his personality was so commanding that Cromwell and others urged him to return to England, and it even was suggested that a special ship be sent to bear him back to his native land. "John Cotton," wrote the grim Carlyle in his own dramatic and effective way, "his mark very curiously stamped on the face of this planet, very likely to continue for some time."

It is hardly necessary to say much in regard to the outward life of this conspicuous Puritan. John Cotton was born in Derbyshire, England, on the fourth day of December, 1585. His parents, so one of his earliest biographers informs us, were "of good reputation; their condition, as to the things of this life, competent; neither unable to defray the expenses of his education in literature, nor so abounding as to be a temptation, on the other hand, unto the neglect thereof." At an early age he was sent to Cambridge University, — "that nursing mother of so many Puritan divines"; and he spent there fifteen studious and profitable years. Chosen Fellow of Emmanuel College after taking his Bachelor Degree, he passed by quick promotion through several important offices, becoming in the first place head lecturer of the famous college, then Dean and Catechist,

JOHN COTTON

while also acting as a tutor. In becoming Fellow he had "taken orders" in the Established Church, as was then the custom and the regulation both at Cambridge and at Oxford, and he soon gave evidence of marked proficiency in the two great lines wherein the deep foundations of his fame were laid, I mean in scholarship and oratory. Cotton was a man of extraordinary learning, but he likewise was a preacher of great rhetorical gifts and power of persuasive and dramatic speech. It is well to understand this at the outset, and to get this latter quality in particular distinctly in our minds. Except for his gifts as a preacher, his capacity for holding people, and even for entrancing them in his sermons, he never would have wielded half the influence of which he came to be possessed. His learning gave him authority, and made men look to him with admiration and respect; but it was in his case, as it has been in the Christian church since the greatest of all preachers spoke the Sermon on the Mount — the men who have shaped the world's theology, and given impulse and direction to social and religious reformations, have been less the thinkers delving amid their books than the exhorters who have gone among the people. The pallid cheeks of the patient scholar are not so much the symbol and the sign of broadening and advancing religious thought as the glowing lips of the eager prophet which have felt the touch of the living fire which was taken from the altar. But here was a man who added to his great attainments in the first direction an unusual power in the second.

The testimony to his learning is both ample and emphatic. "He was proficient in the logic and philosophy then taught in the schools; was a critical master of Greek; and could converse fluently either in Latin or in Hebrew." His power of application must have been remarkable, and it continued with him apparently to the end. "A sand-glass," we are told, "which would run four hours stood near him as he studied, and, being turned over three times, measured his day's work. This he called 'a scholar's day.' He was careful and thorough in preparation for his Sunday work. His sermons were always finished, it appears, by two o'clock on Saturday afternoons; in allusion to which, he once said in rebuking the careless ways of others, 'God will curse that man's labors who lumbers up and down in the world all the week, and then upon Saturday in the afternoon goes to his study.'"

With careful habits such as these it was not unnatural that his reputation for learning was great in his own day, and has survived distinctly ever since. He was spoken of as "a walking encyclopaedia or library," and long years after his death, Dr. Chauncy — a successor in the First Church

JOHN COTTON

pulpit — took occasion once to say of him that "the great Cotton had more learning and understanding than *all* that were descended from him" — a remark, however, let me add, which was made before the day of Phillips Brooks, of Charles Francis Adams, and of William Everett.

With a reputation, then, for scholarship and eloquence already well established, and with marked Puritanical leanings, John Cotton passed in 1612 from his post in Emmanuel College to the work of the active ministry in old Boston, Lincolnshire. He became the vicar of St. Botolph's Church, then, as now, I believe, the largest parish church in England, and a building cathedral-like in appearance and proportions.

The English Boston of to-day is an unattractive and comparatively uninteresting little town, somewhat dirty and markedly decadent, and set down in the flattest and least lovely part of England. A tidal river flows past the provincial city and day by day unblushingly lays bare its muddy and unsightly sides. But above it, dominating not alone the river and the town, but much of the surrounding country, mounts the lordly lantern-tower of the noble church. The church is the centre of the little city, and almost the sole attraction that it has to offer to the ordinary tourist.

And thus it was in still another sense, three centuries ago. For Cotton's ministry was one of power and effectiveness. All classes of the people yielded to his sway. He was busily employed with voice and pen, in public and in private ministrations. The number of the services in the church had to be increased to meet the needs and wishes of the people, and his hearers flocked back from the church to gather round him in his home. He seems to have had a special attraction for students, some of whom came across from Holland and Germany to study with him. In short he soon had made himself one of the very foremost preachers and divines in England. He was only twenty-eight when his ministry began there, and it lasted for a score of fruitful but not particularly peaceful years.

The years, I say, were not entirely peaceful. From the very outset his Puritan tendencies and sympathies were a cause of suspicion and of opposition. Accusations were brought against him on the ground that he refrained from certain rites and omitted the performance of certain ecclesiastical ceremonies. At one time he was forbidden the pulpit while his case was being considered.

But his friends were powerful, and saved him for a time from further discipline and interference. As one of his earlier biographers quaintly puts it, "he found himself healed of his ecclesiastical bronchitis, and restored to the use of his voice in the pulpit." But the flame of opposition had been

JOHN COTTON 25

merely checked, and not extinguished. It soon blazed up again in earnest. And now the influence of neither earls nor bishops was enough to save him; for grim Archbishop Laud had come to power, and, as primate of the Church, was bent on rooting out the Puritan heresy. Cotton was a shining mark, and far too influential to be longer left at large. Charges were preferred against him. Had they been indictments of a "moral nature," relating to "lapses in his personal life or character," his friends declared they might perhaps have saved him. As it was they felt their utter inability to protect him from imprisonment, and probable torture, if not death. He had been too lax in his conformity to churchly ways. Laud had been heard to say on more than one occasion, "Oh, that I might meet with Mr. Cotton!" Flight, therefore, was considered necessary. He thought for a time of taking refuge in Holland. But letters just then opportunely came from Governor Winthrop and the infant church in this other Boston, and he resolved to cross the ocean, and to carve for himself a new career in the town which, partly in his honor, had received its name. Thus England lost one of her greatest scholars and most famous preachers and reformers; and England's loss was a mighty gain for the struggling colony across the sea.

Cotton carried with him on the ship a number of his faithful friends and fond parishioners, and he had as fellow passengers the Rev. Samuel Stone and the Rev. Thomas Hooker. The arrival of these three distinguished men together in Boston harbor gave rise to a humorous saying among the colonists, which shows that our Puritan ancestors were not entirely devoid of pleasantry. It was declared that the colony was now supplied with three of the chief essentials of life. They had *Cotton* for clothing, and *Stone* for building, and *Hooker* for fishing.

John Cotton was in his forty-ninth year when he landed on these shores, and we can hardly exaggerate the joy and satisfaction that his coming brought the colonists. He was a mighty acquisition; a trump-card in their feeble hand; a tower of enormous strength. They had longed for him from the first, and now they felt equipped to fight successfully the arduous battle they had well begun. It was decided at once "that this great light must be set in their chief candlestick," and a few weeks after his arrival, he was appointed teacher of the First Church, of which John Wilson was the pastor.

Thus began his wonderful career in cisatlantic Boston, which, lacking but one year and a little more, was to be as long as his difficult and dramatic ministry in the Boston of old England. But his lot was destined not to be an easy one. New difficulties cropped up in his path, and perplexing questions soon called for settlement. In outward

JOHN COTTON

ways alone, of course, the change was great, and must have cost him many a pang. There, in old England, had been comfort, here was hardship; there was plenty, here privation; there was beauty, here a ragged, untamed wilderness. Instead of the stately church in which he long had labored, he found himself in what could have hardly been much better than a settler's cabin — the walls of which were mostly clay, and the roof of roughest thatch. But conscience, and the sense of rectitude, can glorify the humblest dwelling upon earth, as well as make oppressive and unbearable the fairest and most beautiful surroundings; and conscience had alone conducted him to this new land of labor and self-sacrifice.

Of Cotton's influence upon New England it would be difficult to say too much, and the extent of the power that he wielded cannot easily be over-emphasized. "Whatever John Cotton delivered in the pulpit," wrote a contemporary historian, "was soon put into an order of the court, or set up as a practice in the church." It was Roger Williams' somewhat sardonic comment that "people in Massachusetts could hardly believe that God would suffer Mr. Cotton to err." That it was a stern and almost tyrannical influence which he exerted, goes without our saying it; for those early Puritans were not conspicuous for gentleness, and Cotton was a Puritan in all the tissues of his mind and every fibre of his conscience. It was due to him, much more than to any other single individual, that James Russell Lowell, two centuries later, could describe New England as "all meeting-house when I was growing up." For Cotton was the "Patriarch of the Massachusetts Theocracy." That Theocracy, however, did speedy outrage to the principles of civic liberty, and opened wide the door for intolerance and persecution. It was utterly impossible to carry out in practice, and it gave deliberate denial to the fundamental Protestant principle of the right of private judgment.

It is important to remember, none the less, that the law by which it came to be established was none of Cotton's laying down. Two years before he reached these shores, the General Court had passed this famous resolution: "It is ordered that henceforth no man shall be admitted to the freedom of this Commonwealth but such as are members of the churches within the limits of this jurisdiction." In other words, there were to be no voters except church members, and church members were received only upon approval of the clergy. This made the Puritan minister supreme, and gave him power over matters of civic moment. Church and State were one, and the one was to be the Church. "Such," says a writer, "was the compact, homogeneous, and militant organization now preparing to resist the newest thought of the age. The Puri-

JOHN COTTON

tans had not come out into the American wilderness to offer their new home as shelter to all the unclean birds of Europe. They had not come with a vision of a land where each man might do and think as he pleased. They had come to incarnate in institutions certain definite, rigid convictions, and to prevent any opposing institutions from finding a foothold beside them. They had come to *escape* a tyranny which they had found hateful, and to *establish* a tyranny which they believed beneficent and essential." And it was not long before the persecuted came in turn to persecute, and those who had been driven out of England because of their opinions began to banish people from New England for a similar reason.

The part that Cotton played in these distressing and unlovely matters has been the subject of most careful study and of much discussion. He was accused at the time of "acting with duplicity," and his popularity and power suffered for a season something of a slight eclipse. A present-day historian, who is, no doubt, the most distinguished of Cotton's living descendants, — I refer, of course, to Charles Francis Adams, — has characterized Cotton as the "Inquisitor-in-Chief" of the early colony, adding that he searched out every form of heresy, and exercised a rigid discipline over men's opinions. The same writer also speaks of "an ignominious page in an otherwise worthy life."

And yet, to Cotton's lasting credit and renown, it should never be forgotten that he *began* at least by urging leniency, and standing out for toleration. In the face of all his clerical brethren he deprecated measures of harshness and made as light as possible of growing differences of opinion. Even before his arrival in the Bay, the case of Roger Williams had begun to disturb the peace of the little community; and before he was comfortably settled and at home, the controversy took an ugly form and threatening shape. Cotton and Williams had been friends in England, and Cotton was not faithless to the sacred tie. He did not believe, probably, even at that time, in Roger Williams' right and just contention that "civil magistrates have no jurisdiction over people's religious opinions, so long as the public peace is not disturbed." He did not believe, I say, in this entirely sound and reasonable principle; and yet when Williams was tried and found guilty of "dangerous opinions," and ordered to be banished, Cotton was the *only one* among all the ministers of the Bay who did not vote in favor of the harsh decree. Later on he wrote to Williams that the decree was passed "without his counsel or consent" — although he added, somewhat curiously, that he thought it "righteous in the eyes of God."

Much the same, too, was his attitude and bearing in the midst of the greater and more serious con-

JOHN COTTON

troversy which raged around the teachings and the person of Mrs. Anne Hutchinson. We cannot enter here into all the doctrinal thickets and the metaphysical mazes of that strange and pathetic conflict. Many of the people who took part in it lost their way in a hopeless tangle of unreal words and phrases and distinctions, and hardly knew what it was all about. The only point of importance is this — that Cotton tried to stem the ministerial onrush of persecution and abuse. He poured the oil of his magnetic eloquence upon the troubled waters. He began by making light of the matter, and by acting as if it were not worth men's serious attention. "Tell our trans-Atlantic friends," he said to a ship's company about to depart for England, "that all our strife is about magnifying the grace of God: some seek to exalt the grace of God *towards* us; and some the grace of God *within* us."

When the battle waxed more fierce, he faced again the united front of his clerical brethren, practically all of whom were bitter in their wish to punish the unfortunate woman. Only at the last, when he had spoken on her side, and urged a tolerant treatment, did he let himself be talked around and fall in with the harsher and more narrow notions of his brother clergy.

In ways like these it may be claimed that Cotton showed a lack of vigorous will power, and displayed his incapacity to stand by his convictions. It might appear that he did not have that "rockie strength" for which the founder of the Providence Plantation was so famous.

But that, I think, is not the explanation of the somewhat puzzling facts. It was all, as so often happens in this world, a matter of where the emphasis is placed. Cotton believed in the abstract *policy* of exclusion, but when it came to *practice* his kind heart did not like it. The fact of the matter is that the emphasis which Roger Williams laid on *liberty* was laid by Cotton upon *law* and *order*. He saw the need of a firm and stable government. The least desirable colonists were those who acted as disturbers of the peace. He shared the delusion, likewise, — which was a noble though mistaken dream, — that a compact company of similarly minded believers could be gathered and perpetuated, who should realize and work out for themselves the kingdom of heaven upon earth.

Puritanism, moreover, as we cannot too rigidly remember, was first of all "an *ethical power*. It desired the moral betterment of the people." In the eyes of its divines, purity of life was more important than liberty of action, and strict adherence to the moral law was considered more necessary than individual freedom of belief. It believed, too, in an active and authoritative church, which exercised dominion over men; not indeed, as hap

JOHN COTTON

pened in the Church of England at that time, in regard to rites and churchly ceremonies, but so far as upright living, noble doing, and right believing were concerned. This was part and parcel of its Calvinism, and Cotton was an ardent and devout disciple of the iron autocrat of old Geneva. It was he who made the remark, which has often been quoted, that he "loved to sweeten his mouth with a morsel of Calvin before he went to sleep." "I have read the Fathers," he used to say, "and the Schoolmen, and Calvin, too; but I find that he that has Calvin has them all." Calvin's *Institutes*, however, were hardly less distinctive of him than his well-known *doctrines*, and he labored quite as ardently for purer civic conditions as he strove for ways or forms of thinking and belief. "Calvinism," wrote that graphic historian, James Anthony Froude, who excelled so far in historic insight the men who criticized him for inaccuracy — "Calvinism was the spirit which rises in revolt against untruth, the spirit which has appeared and reappeared, and in due time will appear again, unless God be a delusion and man be as the beasts that perish. For it is but the inflashing upon the conscience with overwhelming force of the nature and origin of the laws which exist, whether we acknowledge them or whether we deny them, and will have their way to our weal or woe, according to the attitude in which we please to place ourselves toward them, . . . not to be altered by us, but to be discerned and obeyed by us at our everlasting peril."[1] "It is astonishing to find," he wrote once to a friend, "how little in ordinary life the Calvinists talked or wrote about doctrine. The doctrine was never more than the dress. The living creature was wholly moral and political."

And thus it was with Cotton. The ends he sought were moral and political, ethical and social. The business of the Church, he held, was to inspire and direct the State. The magistrate was an agent of the Lord. Religion had to do with civic matters.

A Theocracy seemed to him a higher form of government than Democracy. For "if the people are governors," he asked, "who, then, are the governed?" "When a commonwealth hath liberty to mould its own frame, I conceive the Scriptures hath given full directions for the right ordering of the same. It is better that the Commonwealth be fashioned to the setting forth of God's house, which is his church, than to accommodate the church's frame to the civil state." And yet this man, in spite of Theocratic tendencies and practices, was the mighty champion and the stern defender of what is known as the "New England way" in matters of church government. That way was the way of *Congregationalism* — a term, indeed, which Cotton, we are told, originated.

[1] *Short Studies*, 2d series, page 52.

JOHN COTTON

The Congregational way, however, is the way of pure democracy within the church. It meant entire liberty and full equality before the Lord. But what was right and best in *church* could not long be denied the State. And so "the New England way" inevitably broadened out until it led at last and opened into the civic and religious freedom which we now enjoy.

The influence of Cotton in the colony deepened with the years, and grew continually greater. He held an undisputed sway. After the first disturbances with Roger Williams and with Anne Hutchinson were over, and he yielded to the clerical party, there was no abatement in his popularity and power. He was followed, obeyed, admired, worshipped almost. His scholarship and general intellectual attainments set him in a place apart. There were none who could approach him in these high respects.

To these mental gifts, moreover, there was added a singularly sweet and loving disposition. Dignity and gentleness were mingled in him. Righteousness and peace embraced and kissed each other in his character. He had in full degree that grave humility for which the Puritan was famous. Once when a discontented parishioner rebuked him, saying that his ministry was falling off, and was either "dark or flat," he gently answered, "Both, brother," and said no more in his defence.

His generosity, it seems, was likewise marked, and he had a noble scorn of worldly goods. He insisted that his salary should come only from the free-will offerings of his people, and out of his limited resources he gave with handsome hand to others. "In effecting his settlement in New England he had spent a considerable sum of money for those days." But when the people wished to reimburse him, he said that "it was not necessary in the circumstances." He kept open house and practised, it was said, the hospitality of a bishop, paying particular attention to the needy and distressed. On one occasion when news was brought of the suffering condition of the people in a little church in Bermuda, and a contribution from Boston people was solicited, it was noted that no one exceeded, and only one person equalled, the generous amount that was given by the teacher of the church.

It is probable, however, as I hinted at the outset, that he owed his extraordinary influence more to his wonderful pulpit eloquence than to any other quality. For John Cotton first and foremost was a *preacher*. He bewitched and swayed the undergraduates at old Cambridge when himself but a youth of hardly more than twenty-five. He filled the great church of St. Botolph to the doors with a hungry multitude who listened to his passionate and pleading words; and, when he came to these forbidding shores the joyful people clustered round him, and not only gave attention to his words, but put his precepts into practice.

Longfellow, in his *New England Tragedies*, using words that an early writer had employed, describes him as "Chrysostom in the pulpit; Augustine in disputation; Timothy in his home!" adding:

> The Lantern of St. Botolph's ceased to burn
> When from the portals of that church he came
> To be a burning and a shining light
> Here in the wilderness.

The tributes, or the testimonies, on this point are numerous, and too definite and clear to leave us any room for doubt. He belongs in the category of the world's great preachers. A contemporary writer, speaking of him, declared that he "had such an insinuating and melting way in his preaching that he would usually carry his very adversary captive after the triumphant chariot of his rhetoric."

Another writer of the time, in trying to express his feelings, found the resources of prose entirely inadequate for his purpose, and burst forth thus into very doubtful verse:

> A man of might at heavenly eloquence
> To fix the ear and charm the conscience;
> As if Apollos were revived in him,
> Or he had learnèd of a Seraphim.

. . . .

Rocks rent before him; blind received their sight;
Souls leveled to the dunghill stood upright.

It has been remarked more than once by careful students of the subject that Cotton's printed sermons give no evidence of this extraordinary power. They are dry, scholastic, and uninteresting — lighted up by no dramatic illustrations, and brightened by no pithy sayings. They are the dullest, heaviest, and most unexhilarating reading at the present time that one can well imagine.

Yet in all of this there is nothing fairly to be called exceptional, unless it be in matter of degree. The same has been the case with other mighty preachers whose power with their hearers has been more marked and wonderful than Cotton's. It was thus with Whitefield, for example. If you read the printed sermons of Whitefield it is hard to understand the countless multitudes who sat or stood upon the hillsides in all kinds of weather when he preached in the open air; and who climbed up to the roofs of churches, and stood outside the open windows, and even filled the neighboring squares and streets, when he spoke within some building. The sermons of the famous Methodist that were written out, or taken down and given to the press, do not disclose much more than those of Cotton where the secret of the preacher's power lay. The simple fact of the matter is that elements exist in all such cases which never can be set in type, or struck off in the printer's ink — the tones of a voice, the flash of a radiant eye, the expression of a rapt and pious countenance, the magnetic personality, which oftentimes exert hypnotic influence. Such elements as these, no doubt, were prominent and well developed in the case of Cotton, while the sermons that he put into print were probably his most scholastic and didactic.

As regards "the manner of his preaching," we are told that "he was plain and perspicuous. He consistently forebore to make any display of his vast learning in the pulpit. He addressed himself to the common people. His chief anxiety was to be understood. He would often say: 'I desire to speak so as to be understood by the meanest capacity.'"

His voice, it seems from what has been reported of him, was clear and distinct, not loud; and he could make himself heard with ease in the largest auditorium. There was such life and vigor and alertness in his preaching that his colleague, Mr. Wilson, once said: "One almost thinks that he hears the very prophet speak, upon whose words he is dwelling."

His popularity and power, after the first, never suffered any abatement or decline. He died as he had lived, — faithful, fervent, public-spirited, devout, and conscientious, — a Puritan who suffered more than many for his principles, a leader who was privileged to guide and stimulate the elect. Carlyle was right. His mark is very definitely, if not curiously, stamped on the face of this planet, very likely to continue for some time. Two centuries and more have not effaced it, but have rather brought its living and ennobling lines into greater clearness; and it may be that when two centuries more have fled, the people will still tell about his wisdom, and the congregation will show forth his praise.

His brother ministers, so we are told, lifted him aloft in death, and bore his body on their shoulders to the tomb. So we, after all this lapse of years, would lift him up once more in admiration and respect, that we may bear him forward, not into the darkness and the silence of the tomb, but into that bright and lasting radiance of earthly immortality which belongs to the greatest and the purest sons of men.

His descendants in the seventh and eighth generations have offered to the church of which he was the first and greatest teacher a fitting and beautiful memorial, praying that in their day they may be as faithful to the mighty and eternal trusts of life as their famous ancestor revealed himself in his. As his immediate successor in the pulpit wrote at the close of his little memoir, from which

I have quoted more than once already: "It is not material in what age we live; but that we live as we ought in that age wherein we live."

"*Moriar ego morte justorum, et sit finis meus sicut illius.*"

JOHN FISKE AGAIN

JOHN FISKE AGAIN

THE strange and sudden outburst against the teaching of Evolution, which has unexpectedly declared itself in the United States, directs attention once again toward the actual bearing of scientific thought upon religious truth. We find ourselves recalling the panic that occurred and the discussions that took place when Darwin's *Origin of Species* was first given to the world. A perfect storm of protest was the quick result. Devout believers saw the Bible set at naught, and proclaimed all those who accepted the new teachings as utter atheists. From that time on, endless essays and volumes of learned books were written, all bearing upon the general subject of the warfare between Science and Religion, or Theology. In 1896, Andrew D. White published two ponderous volumes on the subject, which ought forever to have settled the question; but it was not so easily to be put to rest. The battle went on fiercely for a number of years, with many casualties on both sides, but with the tide of victory setting steadily against superstition, dogma, and irrational belief. At last a truce was called, which had all the appearance of meaning peace. The wise and discerning came to the conclusion that there really was no necessary conflict between the two, and that there never should have been any. The truth at length emerged from the minds of those who, having minds, knew how to use them, that Religion had nothing to fear and much to gain from the marvellous revelations that Science had to offer.

It was more than a generation since that this intellectual armistice was achieved. Had anyone at that time ventured to predict that, after a full fourth of the twentieth century had become a part of recorded history, the pathetic controversy would again break forth; that "Monkey and Man" books would again be written in answer to a popular demand; and that laws would actually be passed in the United States forbidding the teaching of Evolution in the Public Schools, and that these laws would be enforced — why, forty years ago, a person prophesying such impossible things would have been considered a proper candidate for careful seclusion. We should have turned our back on him, if we had gone even to that much trouble, believing him to deserve no more than mere contempt. And yet, the prediction which would have seemed supremely silly has definitely and dramatically come to pass. America, which has boasted so freely of the benefits of universal education and has claimed to be the most enlightened country in the world, with the least amount of illiteracy in proportion to population, has come to be a laughing-stock in the eyes of such effete countries as France and England, where scholars wonder what the meaning is of all this fuss. Perhaps, as we in turn permit ourselves to wonder also, we may be pardoned if we call to mind a witticism on the part of the famous Sydney Smith. "The further I travel west," remarked the eminent Canon of St. Paul's Cathedral, "the more convinced I am that the 'Wise men' came from the East."

Without more ado, however, I may venture to call attention to a writer who rendered very signal service in his day, by calling eloquent attention to the spiritual implications of modern Science in general and of Evolution in particular.

Some years ago I was sitting in the corridor of a European hotel talking with an Englishwoman. She was a person of culture and education, and not without a certain literary stimulus, for she was a sister of John Cross who became the husband of George Eliot. A batch of home letters was in my hand. One of them chanced to be from John Fiske in regard to some lecture engagement, and something prompted me to show my companion the beautifully clear and distinct signature. She stared at it, however, as blankly as if the name had been that of Henry Smith or James Jones. She had never heard of the author of *Cosmic Philosophy* and the *Destiny of Man*.

My amazement at the time was somewhat great; but stranger things have happened to me since, and I have ceased to feel resentment at this slight upon a great man's reputation. On the day after Lowell's death, for instance, I chanced to sit at an English luncheon table near Stopford Brooke. As was natural, the conversation turned to Lowell's life and work, and Mr. Brooke ventured his opinion that the great American, whom he had met and known in London, was a brilliant essayist, but no poet. "You Americans," he said, "enjoy his verses because he appeals to your patriotism."

Somewhat nettled by the criticism, I asked him what he did with the *Vision of Sir Launfal*, quoting at the same time a line or two. But the English Man of Letters, at that time one of the greatest living authorities in English literature, had never even heard of the poem.

It is not of Lowell, however, but of Fiske, that I would try to speak; and more especially of the contribution that he made to religious thought. The little incident alluded to is hardly indicative of the actual facts, I think; for John Fiske really had a European reputation. The scholarly and thoughtful of other lands than ours knew his

JOHN FISKE AGAIN

work and valued it. He was the intimate personal friend of many of the men who, fifty years ago, were the leaders of English thought.

That he was a man of marvellous intellectual gifts it is hardly necessary to assert. Unlike many great men, of whom it is written for our comfort that they were dull and backward in their youth, Fiske was remarkably precocious from the first. "At seven he had read a large part of Cæsar, and was reading Rollin, Josephus, and Goldsmith's *History of Greece*. Before he was nine he had read nearly all of Shakespeare, and much of Milton, Bunyan, and Pope. He began Greek at nine. By eleven he had read Gibbon, Robertson, and Prescott, and most of Froissart, and he wrote from memory a chronological table from B.C. 1000 to A.D. 1820, filling a quarto blank-book of 60 pages. At thirteen he had read the whole of Virgil, Horace, Tacitus, Sallust, Suetonius, and much of Livy, Cicero, Ovid, Catullus, and Juvenal. At the same time he had gone through Euclid, plane and spherical trigonometry, surveying and navigation, and analytical geometry, and was well advanced in differential calculus. At fifteen he could read Plato and Herodotus at sight, and was beginning German. Within the next year he was keeping his diary in Spanish, and was reading French, Italian, and Portuguese. He began Hebrew at seventeen, and took up Sanskrit the next year. . . . He averaged twelve hours study daily, twelve months of the year, before he was sixteen, and afterwards, nearly fifteen hours daily, working with persistent energy. After graduating from Harvard with honors in 1863, he entered the Harvard Law School, and in one year he had imbibed sufficient legal information to gain admittance to the Suffolk Bar." Such intellectual exploits make ordinary mortals feel like laying by the spear and hanging up the sword in sheer discouragement, if not despair.

We are not concerned, however, with Mr. Fiske's career in general, but only with its bearing on religion. My own connection with his religious utterances is perhaps significant. It was our custom in New Bedford to have him come each year to the First Congregational Society and deliver an address, which took the place of the Sunday morning sermon. All the chapters in his little book *Through Nature to God* were read from the New Bedford pulpit, which is a distinction, I believe, to which hardly another church in the country can lay claim. The fact itself is an evidence both of the freedom of the modern pulpit and of the religious tendencies of John Fiske's mind.

To these tendencies, however, the very books of the man, with their familiar titles, bear clear and unmistakable testimony. It surely was not accidental that almost the very first book he published was called *The Unseen World*, and that among the last was the little volume on *Life Everlasting*. Nor, between the two, throughout the period of his active intellectual life, did he ever lose his interest in things divine, or permanently remove his gaze from the things invisible. He might write history; but his history was also prophecy. He might give himself to science; but he never left his science unattended by his faith. Although he dealt with "Myths" and the "makers" of them, he was conscious still of the "Everlasting Reality of Religion" which lies deep down beneath all mythical accretions. When he sought for the roots of the various languages of the world, he did not forget those universal instincts of the race which no speech can utter and no language frame.

Thus it may be frankly said, I think, and said with truth, that the natural attitude of John Fiske's mind was a religious attitude. And it was religious for two reasons. First, because, as Josiah Royce reminded us, he kept his simple, natural, childish instincts and desires strong and fresh. He was always sensitive to beauty — quick to the feelings of awe and reverence. The training and discipline of the scholar never silenced the music of his soul. Then, in the second place, which is almost as important, Fiske never allowed himself to become confined in any narrow compartment of the universe. He did not stoop so low upon the shore of life, to study minute grains of truth, that he became unconscious of the sweeping billows from God's infinite ocean, as they break in glory at our feet.

He had a scholar's love of accuracy, and he paid the greatest respect to scientific and historic details. But these were means, not ends; foundation stones, not finished temples. There was a natural and instinctive largeness in his view of things. It is significant that his first piece of published writing was an article dealing with Buckle's *History of Civilization*. The book apparently interested him because of its inclusive character. And this tendency showed itself in little ways as well as large ones. His brother-in-law, Mr. James Brooks, told me once how he came up to Petersham for a little rest, after a long period of protracted work. As he sat down upon the veranda and looked off across the valley to the rolling hills beyond, he clasped his hands in front of his immense corporeal form — no easy task in his later years — and said with a sigh, "I should like to sit here for a million years." That was the man; wrapt in contented wonder before the marvels of God's creation, and extending the thoughts of a summer evening to a period of a million years.

We have, however, Mr. Fiske's own words in witness of the early and lifelong interest that he took

JOHN FISKE AGAIN

in religious and theological questions. "When I was fourteen years old," he says of himself, "a scheme had begun to dawn vaguely on my mind" to prepare "a work on the true nature of Christianity." These words were written in 1885, and the scheme seems never to have faded completely from his mind.

In *The Unseen World*, published first in 1876, after apologizing for the meagre treatment of so large and important a subject as the "Jesus of History," he said in a footnote: "These defects I hope to remedy in a future work on 'Jesus of Nazareth, and the Founding of Christianity,' for which the present articles must be regarded as furnishing only a few introductory hints. This work has been for several years on my mind; but, as it may still be long before I can find the leisure needful for writing it out, it seemed best to republish these preliminary sketches." [1]

Ten years later he repeated the same statement, and renewed his promise. He said in the Preface of the *Idea of God*, referring to his *Destiny of Man*: "The two books, taken together, contain the bare outlines of a theory of Religion which I earnestly hope at some future time to state elaborately. . . . Such a book . . . requires long and varied preparation; and I have always regarded my other books . . . as simply wayside studies preliminary to the

[1] *The Unseen World*, page 66.

undertaking of this complicated and difficult task." [1]

Had Fiske lived longer, it might have been with him as it was with James Martineau. For in 1836, when he was just turned thirty, the English philosopher promised the world a volume dealing with the question, "What is Christianity?" In more than one of the prefaces of his subsequent books he assured his readers that his purpose was still firm. Not until 1890, however, more than half a century later, at the age of eighty-five, did he make the promise good.

Such contribution, therefore, as Fiske actually made to religion is only a part of what he clearly had in mind. We can only vaguely imagine how all the wealth of his historical studies, to which he devoted the best years of his life, would have gone to strengthen and to clarify that "Theory of Religion" which he vaguely outlined in his youth.

Now, the contribution which John Fiske made to religion was, in its general character, very similar to the contribution which he made to the theory and philosophy of evolution. It was not unlike, too, the contribution that he made to history. There was a wonderful unity in his work, despite the different fields in which he labored. These contributions were, first, general, and second, definite and specific.

[1] *The Idea of God*, Preface, page xxx.

JOHN FISKE AGAIN

It has been said, for instance, and said with truth, that Fiske's great mission was "to take the Darwinian theory and carry it on to a higher plane; to stamp the evolutionary philosophy with the impress of more spiritual thought . . . than was given it by Darwin, or by Huxley and Tyndall. He discovered a higher and finer significance in the theory than Darwin himself had dreamed" it contained. He carried out that theory, too, and gave it a broad and wholesome application, following in the footsteps of Herbert Spencer. He walked upon much higher levels, however, than were ever trodden by the feet of the great philosopher of evolution; and, unlike his master, whose gaze was so often earthward, his eyes were always fastened on the stars. He was willing to wait for a million years, too, while the processes of God were being completed.

In addition, however, to this general service in the cause of evolution he made that distinct and important contribution which is now so very familiar. He was evidently proud of it, as indeed he had good cause to be. Again and again in his different volumes he refers to it as his, almost as if he feared the world would forget its origin — which might, indeed, have been the case. This special contribution was, of course, the importance of the prolonged period of infancy in the human offspring. In a speech which he made at a dinner given in his honor in New York in 1895, Mr. Fiske unfolded the biography of this discovery, telling how the idea first was born in his mind, slowly grew, and finally took shape and became mature. It is an interesting story; but we need not repeat it here. Nor is it necessary to enlarge upon the nature and value of the contribution itself. We are all familiar with it.

It contributed, indeed, to much more than evolution; for, like every other really great and important truth, it has its bearing upon ethics and religion. It traces deep into fruitful soil the cosmic roots of love and self-sacrifice, and it places in the human heart the very feel of the Divine.

Let us speak more definitely, however, of his distinctive contribution to religion.

It cannot be said that he originated for religion any single truth of like importance to this one great thought which he proudly, and yet reverently, laid on the altar of the doctrine of evolution. Yet he served the cause of faith in more ways, both direct and indirect, than can ever be fully known or definitely measured. What a tower of strength it was, for instance, — and for the matter of that, still is, — to have a man of his acknowledged scholarship and ability and scientific equipment standing boldly forth on the side of spiritual realities. When people were perplexed and science-tossed, wondering whether it was still pos-

JOHN FISKE AGAIN

sible to believe in evolution and also to believe in God and the immortal life, this follower of Darwin and Herbert Spencer lifted up his voice in the cause of faith. His notes of affirmation were as clear and inspiring as the music of the mountaineer's horn upon the Alps, waking the sleepers to behold the dawn. "The presence of God is the one all-pervading fact of life," men heard him say. "I believe it can be shown," he declared before the scholars of the Phi Beta Kappa at Harvard, "that one of the strongest implications of the doctrine of evolution is the everlasting Reality of Religion." And "apart from all questions of revelation," he added, "the light of nature affords us sufficient ground for maintaining that Religion is fundamentally true and must endure." [1]

His trumpet never gave forth an uncertain sound. It must have encouraged him from his higher mental elevation to hear his words caught up and echoed on among the clustering forms of his ardent followers.

How sublime and beautiful were some of his deep-toned utterances! "The Deity revealed in the presence of Evolution," he wrote, "is the ever-present God without whom not a sparrow falls to the ground, and whose voice is heard in each whisper of conscience, even while his splendor dwells in the white ray from yonder star that

[1] *Through Nature to God*, page 150.

began its earthward flight while Abraham's shepherds watched their flocks."[1] And again he declared: "Humanity is not a mere local incident in an endless and aimless series of cosmical changes. . . . There is a Purpose in the world, whereof it is our highest duty to learn the lesson, however well or ill we may fare in rendering a scientific account of it. Thou canst not by searching find out God: yet put thy trust in Him, and against thee the gates of Hell shall not prevail."[2]

These, and others like them, were the affirmations that came to people in their doubts, straight from the searching, scientific mind of Fiske, and gave them strength. "If he can believe in these things still, then we can, too," they said in substance to themselves.

He was equally outspoken, too, in opposition to Rationalism. He referred impatiently to the flippant ease with which people dispose of the greatest questions, in crass ignorance of the very nature of the problem to be solved. He found a good illustration of what he meant in the remark of the astronomer Lalande, that he "had swept the entire heavens with his telescope and found no God." "This," Fiske said, "and the dictum of the physiologist, 'no thought without phosphorus,' I am inclined to think . . . are the two remarks

[1] *Through Nature to God*, page 150.
[2] *The Idea of God*, page 167.

JOHN FISKE AGAIN

most colossal in their silliness that ever appeared in print."[1]

Of the general service that Fiske rendered Religion in these ways I do not believe too much can ever be said. He helped to stem the tide of doubt and materialism which set in with so strong a current a generation since. He assured people that the citadel of faith was still secure, and that only the outer walls of unimportant dogma have fallen before the artillery of Science. "That inward conviction," he declared, — referring to belief in God, — "is itself one of the master facts of the universe, and as much entitled to respect as any fact in physical nature can possibly be."[2] The "Darwinian theory," he said, when "properly understood, replaces as much Teleology as it destroys." And, "for my own part," he wrote, "I believe in the Immortality of the Soul, not in the sense in which I accept the demonstrable truths of Science, but as a supreme act of faith in the reasonableness of God's work."[3]

That Fiske allowed his heart to influence his head in these matters is undoubtedly a fact. In his later years, which were certainly his richest and fullest, he permitted himself to overstep the narrow limits he had set for himself in the early period of his cosmic philosophy. He was never contented

[1] *Through Nature to God*, page 140.
[2] *Ibid.*, page vii.
[3] *The Destiny of Man*, page 113.

to stand still. His contribution to religious thought was distinctly cumulative. As the years sped by, his faith increased. The more widely he read, and the more deeply he thought, the more confidently he believed. His friends were not prepared for this development, and some of them at first could hardly understand it.

Martineau set down in the Preface to his *Study of Religion* a remark that was made by an English representative of the Positivist School of Philosophy when he first was told of the conclusions set forth in *The Destiny of Man*. "What? John Fiske say that?" the disciple of Compte exclaimed. "Well, it only proves, what I have always maintained, that you cannot make the slightest concession to Metaphysics, without ending in a theology." [1] A remark, adds Martineau, which frankly admits that "if you once allow yourself to think about the origin and the end of things, you will have to believe in a God and Immortality."

Speaking now in a more specific way, let us ask what Fiske had to offer us that was really new and helpful and constructive. We may consider, first, his contribution to our thought concerning the being of God and his nature, and secondly, the importance of what he suggested concerning the nature of man and his destiny.

That Fiske was no Agnostic, but a distinct be-

[1] *The Destiny of Man*, page 116.

JOHN FISKE AGAIN

liever in God, even if not — in the ordinary sense of the word — an ardent worshipper, is evident. "It probably never occurred to any one," he wrote, "to try to prove the existence of a God until it was doubted; and doubts on that subject are very modern. Omitting from the account a few score of ingenious Philosophers, it may be said that all mankind, the wisest and the simplest, have taken for granted the existence of a Deity. . . . Such a postulate," he added, in his lecture on the "Everlasting Reality of Religion," "has formed a part of all human thinking from primitive ages down to the present time."[1]

In this same lecture, which forms a part of his little volume *Through Nature to God*, he brought forward and elaborated an argument to *prove* the existence of God, which he claimed was wholly new and original.

The argument is this: "Every stage of enlargement in life has had reference to, and has been brought about by, actual existences outside." The eye, for instance, with its wonderful power of sight, was developed by the force of light acting upon some sensitive spot in the organism of the living creature. The ear, in a similar fashion, was developed "in response to the outward existence of acoustic vibration; the mother's love came in response to the infant's needs; fidelity and honor

[1] *Through Nature to God*, pages 163-164.

were slowly developed as the nascent social life required them: everywhere the internal adjustment has been brought about so as to harmonize with some actually existing external fact. Such has been nature's method, such is the deepest law of life that science has been able to detect."

Now, at a critical time in the history of our planet, we find "the nascent Human soul vaguely reaching forth toward something akin to itself, not in the realm of fleeting phenomena, but in the eternal presence beyond. An internal adjustment of ideas was achieved in correspondence with an unseen world." As the eye came in answer to the force of light, and the ear was developed by the presence of sound, so the soul of man in reaching up toward spiritual things has been relating itself to spiritual force, which is the very cause and explanation of the Soul's existence. "If the relation thus established in the morning twilight of man's existence between the human soul and a world invisible and immaterial is a relation of which only the subjective term is real, and the objective term is non-existent, then, I say, it is something utterly without precedent in the whole history of creation." And he adds, "All the analogies of Evolution, so far as we have yet been able to decipher it, are overwhelmingly against any such supposition."

Such is the argument of which Fiske could write:

"So far as I am aware it is here advanced for the first time." Of course he did not claim for it anything like scientific demonstration. As "an appeal to our common sense," however, he did feel that it had tremendous weight, and he considered it "far more convincing than any chain of subtle metaphysical reasoning can ever be." And in this he probably was right. To the best of my knowledge, however, the argument has never played any important part on the stage of philosophic thought. After being confidently and glowingly introduced, it found no special favor, and apparently has been retired to that quiet corner where so many other arguments of similar pretensions may be found. Meanwhile the active and absorbing play of doubt and faith proceeds. Mr. Fiske, however, undoubtedly thought well of it, and hoped, perhaps, that here was an important contribution to Theology, to match in significance his contribution to Evolutionary thought. But such is not the case. Its actual value is indicated by his own words. In closing the argument he made appeal to the "Analogies of Evolution." "All the analogies of Evolution," he declared, "are against the supposition that the soul is the only term in the relationship." That single phrase reveals the weight of the argument. It has the lightness of analogy in general, and makes that ever-tempting and fascinating leap from the material to the spiritual. It undertook to carry over "Natural Law" into the "Spiritual World."

Better than this, or than any other definite argument, in fact, was his little book on *The Idea of God*, which brought indeed to many people a wholly new "Idea" of Deity.

It was time for people to be reminded — and among them thoughtful and scientific people — that the old magnified-man Theism had been outgrown, only to give place to cosmic Theism. Denial did not mean destruction, but fulfilment. And he showed "a more excellent way" of looking upon the world, and upon God in relation to the world.

None of his religious writings, however, had the originality or the importance of *The Destiny of Man*. That was the first of what became a series of little volumes, and it remained the best. A prophecy of man's destiny viewed in the light of his origin, it was also a proof of God's being as evidenced by his purposes. For, as Fiske himself well stated in another connection, "It is profoundly true that a theory of things may seem theistic or atheistic in virtue of what it says of man, no less than in virtue of what it says of God."

The conclusion of the book is not its only important part; and to some it may almost appear the least logical and significant. We are told and shown that "the glorious consummation toward

JOHN FISKE AGAIN

which organic evolution is tending is the production of the highest and most perfect psychical life." That being so, the thing we may confidently count upon is "the continued progress of psychical development for future humanity on earth." To infer from the facts a conscious continuance of these psychical qualities after death, was natural, but somewhat visionary.

However that may be, I think we were all gravely disappointed in his final word upon the mighty theme. The little posthumous volume on the *Life Everlasting* was not the climax that we had looked for to the noble prophecies that had gone before. It almost seemed as if when he came to speak directly of a great religious subject, such faith as he had took cover, and suddenly disappeared. He was at home on his native heath of evolutionary analogy. He was bold to declare in a negative way that the faith was not irrational, nor groundless; but — that was almost all. The direct reason of our disappointment lies, of course, in this — that he confined his thought within such narrow limits. He set himself the task of examining nothing more than the objections which have been alleged, in the name of Science, against the validity of the belief. And even within the limits of this somewhat sterile field he wanders away from the central interest, and sends his thoughts into corners of research that contain small inspiration. When we wait to gain some assurance of an Everlasting Life from a philosopher who had once assured his readers that he believed "in the Immortality of the soul as a supreme act of faith in the reasonableness of the world," it is somewhat disappointing to be reminded of Descartes' revolt against the Scholastic Philosophy, and of Newton's contributions to Science. When we hope for eloquent words giving his grounds for faith, we feel no elation in being reminded that Galileo was commanded by the Mediæval church to hold his tongue. Perhaps the abundant satisfaction given by his other books had led people to expect too much; but at any rate they were disappointed. His only conclusion was that "we are at perfect liberty to treat the question of man's Immortality in the disinterested spirit of the naturalist"; and that, "in the course of evolution, there is no more philosophical difficulty in man's acquiring immortal life than in his acquiring the erect posture, and articulate speech."

From the inadequacy of this final word, however, we turn back with joy and satisfaction to that which went before and still abides, a living contribution to religious thought. And yet it may fairly be questioned whether this contribution is likely to be of permanent importance.

Professor A. B. Hart has said, as regards his service to History, that Fiske after all has "done

JOHN FISKE AGAIN

no more than to tell better what other men toiled painfully to tell as best they could." He adds that he lacked the element of original discovery of truth, and that "his most striking generalizations always leave me asking, 'Did he go to the bottom of a subject?' His work, therefore, will not be accepted as foundations on which future historians will build."

Almost the same may be said of Fiske's religious service. His aim was reconciliation, not construction — at least, so far as fundamentals were concerned. His work was that of a bridge-builder. He helped to span with a substantial structure the chasm that yawned in his day — or that seemed to yawn — between Science and Religion. He did not construct a new temple of Religious Faith; nor did he lay the full foundations for such a temple. He merely declared that such a temple was possible, — a new one, — grander and more sublime than any that the past had reared, and he indicated the nature of the material that should be used in its construction.

The theology of the present day, as well as the religion, is in a most chaotic condition. It is without form and void. We are so fearful of dogmas and so fully warned against final statements, that the water of sentiment covers for the most part the earth of our beliefs. What we await is a shaping hand that shall set apart the solid land, and give us something on which to plant our feet securely.

That Fiske in any sense accomplished this will not be claimed. But he made more easy its final accomplishment by someone else. There is permanent value and deep significance in the fact of the "growing predominance of the psychical life" which he unfolded in his *Destiny of Man;* in the historic contrast between the old and the new Theism, which he emphasized in *The Idea of God;* and in the cosmic roots of love and self-sacrifice which he brought to light in *Through Nature to God.* After all, Fiske's actual contribution to Religion consisted of what he believed to be the higher implication of Evolution when rightly understood, and these may be stated very briefly.

All religions, he believed, agree in two assertions, one of speculative and the other of ethical importance. "The first of these assertions is the proposition that the things and events of the world do not exist or occur blindly, but are the orderly manifestations of a Divine Power." And the second is the proposition that "men ought to do certain things, and ought to refrain from doing certain other things," the reason for these ethical distinctions being connected more or less distinctly with the nature and existence of this Divine Power.

Those, he declared, are the essential truths of Religion of all religions, wherever sought and

JOHN FISKE AGAIN

found; and it became his mission to show that the doctrine of Evolution, when rightly understood, asserts and reiterates them both. "It asserts," he tells us over and over again, "as the widest and deepest truth which the study of nature can disclose to us, that there exists a Power to which no limit in time or space is conceivable," of which the phenomena of the universe are only so many manifestations. And this assertion is, to his mind, "identical with the assertion of an Eternal Power, not ourselves, that forms the speculative basis of all Religions."

Nor was it different with the Ethical Sanction which Religion has connected with this belief. It was clear to him that "when you say of a moral belief or a moral sentiment, that it is a product of Evolution, you imply that it is something which the universe through untold ages has been laboring to bring forth, and you ascribe to it a value proportionate to the enormous effort it has cost to produce it." He found and showed us the "principles of right living, which it is man's highest function to put into practice, wrought into the very fibers of the universe," and he could say: "The theoretical sanction thus given," by Evolution, "to right living is incomparably the most powerful that has ever been assigned in any Philosophy of Ethics."

Add to this, his brilliant suggestion that the

"growing predominance of the psychical life" in man encourages belief in Immortality, and you have John Fiske's contribution to Religion — a contribution at once original, brilliant, suggestive, and constructive.

It was given him to make our faith more easy; and we may call him the friend and aider of those who lived in doubt. As such, his works may be cordially commended to a generation just ignorantly warned anew, in the supposed interest of religion, to beware of scientific truth.

JOHN RUSKIN

JOHN RUSKIN

AMERICANS are disposed to find amusement in the strictly limited area of the British Isles. Having themselves a country that reaches from one great ocean to the other, and with rivers that make the Thames and the Tweed look like brooks, or streamlets, they have taken occasion to speak derisively of a little land which "yesterday" you might have motored through, and which "a watch in the night" would enable you to pass over in an aeroplane. But in proportion as the land is small, the scenes and memorials of its great and famous men are many and conspicuous. The schoolboy who complained of American history that it was "all cluttered up with Adamses" might equally well complain that he could not travel far in England without being held up by the birthplace or home or grave of some famous author, reformer, statesman, or inventor. This truth was brought home to me last summer in the course of a motor trip through a part of England and of Scotland.

A first holdup, of an unexpected character, was at the little town of Grantham on the Great North Road. Sallying forth in the early morning, —

which seems to be the only period of the day when motor travelers can secure a little exercise on foot, — I found myself confronted in the public square with a statue of Newton. Not being well informed in regard to the haunts and home of the famous physicist, and wondering whether he had romped as a boy among the apple orchards of Grantham, I sought enlightenment of a tradesman whose drapery shop fronted on the statue in the square. The man looked intelligent — which was why I accosted him. But his education was surely limited, for when I enquired whether Newton had been born in Grantham, or had lived there, apologizing in the same breath for being so ill informed, I quickly discovered a brother in ignorance — only a bigger and an older brother. His answer to my question was brief and definite: "I don't know, sir; I was not acquainted with the gentleman."

But that is not a typically English condition of mind, and much less Scotch. Not only does one find the haunts and homes of great men numerous, and never many miles apart, but the amazing thing is the multitude of visitors that they attract. Finding myself in Edinburgh again, after a period of more than thirty years, I was not unprepared to find the tourists at Abbotsford more numerous than they were in 1892. A few days later, Ayr came upon us by surprise; but it was no surprise to find that Burns's cottage and the other local

JOHN RUSKIN

shrines had more visitors than flock into Stratford-on-Avon of a summer! Another place that lay in our motor path was Ecclefechan, where the stone mason's cottage may be seen which was the birthplace and early home of Thomas Carlyle. We might have gone to Craigenputtock, to see what reasons Jane Welsh had for her complaints, for the place was not far off. But the Lake region with its familiar haunts was near at hand, and we pushed on there to join the fluttering tourists in Dove Cottage, and the tired ones who climbed to Rydal Mount. Not many people, however, who find themselves in the Lake region take the trouble to leave the beaten track and cross lakes and hills in order to pay their respects to Brantwood. Perhaps one reason why Ruskin chose the place was the fact that it was somewhat apart from the restless tide of travel, and not merely because it gave a glorious view of the Coniston Old Man.

Once before, — and on that occasion with a letter from Charles Eliot Norton, — I had gone to Coniston, and finding my way to Brantwood, had been shown the priceless Turners. But this year, when I reached the little town, I was told the astounding news in the first shop that I entered: "Brantwood has just been advertised for sale." Announcement had been seen in the local newspaper! And when I expressed amazement and chagrin, I was informed that it never would have happened had Mrs. Severn lived. I had forgotten about her death. "Yes, she died more than a year ago; and had been buried in the little cemetery behind the Church; close beside the Master to whom she had given so much care." "Joanna's Care," it will be remembered, was the title to one of the chapters of *Præterita*.

All this was a year ago, and whether or not by this time Brantwood has been sold, is a point on which I have no information. But if it has been disposed of, it is much to be regretted. In the first place, it was the solemn wish of Mr. Ruskin — set down in his will, so I was told — that the property should be kept intact. In the second place, it is almost certain that Ruskin's fame will recover from what is probably only a temporary eclipse. And when that happens, the world will wonder why the home of his maturer years was ever lost to the nation in whose golden book his name was long ago indelibly inscribed.

For my own part, I incline to doubt whether justice ever has been fully done to the author of *Modern Painters*, who also wrote a little book called *Unto this Last*, and who opened the eyes of the world to many more precious and enduring things than Turner's pictures. Theodore Parker was accustomed to "thank God for the sun, the moon, and the stars, and for Ralph Waldo Emerson"; and if we are to sing a hallelujah chorus to

JOHN RUSKIN

the glory of mountain peaks and meadow paths, and the floating clouds that wreathe them in celestial glory, we may wisely sing the praises also of the poet-soul who revealed them in their fullness to our clouded understanding.

Stephen Paget, who established a literary reputation by his *Confessio Medici*, confessed to many matters quite unmedical. Among other things he ventured to call Ruskin "The Master of us all; the greatest prophet except Shakespeare that we ever had; whose judgment of us and our work is of everlasting authority." In justification of these encomiums this man of science declared, "He saw through and through externalities into the heart of things, and the spirit of his teaching will endure till the world is too cold for us and our works, and London comes to the natural end of its existence." [1]

It has to be confessed, however, that it is no easy task to measure Ruskin, whether in respect to what he was in himself or as related to the various fields of thought and life in which he labored. His service was unique. Whether or not the niche which he occupies is above that of most of his famous contemporaries, or only widely separated from them, is a point still open to discussion. It is no easy task to classify him rightly, or even to decide his place in the *Tribuna* of the world's long portrait gallery.

[1] Paget, *I Sometimes Think*, page 87.

Above the mantelpiece in the preachers' room at Harvard University might be seen some years ago the photographs of three distinguished men. Two of these men are often associated in our minds. Their friendship built itself into literature, and no one doubts the prophetic influence and value of their words. But many people in their ignorance, or prejudice, might question the right of the third person to be classed with the other two.

The three men of whose photographs I speak are Emerson, Carlyle, and Ruskin. In a merely outward sense there was a deep connection between these great men. They were all social reformers, all heretics in religion, yet all intense believers in the everlasting laws of right. The connecting link between them personally was Carlyle. The great Scotsman had no warmer friend than Emerson, and he gave to none of his English friends such unstinted praise as he gave to Ruskin. "Midst all the din and confused babble of tongues," he wrote, "there rises one clear voice telling truth, where others speak lies, the voice of Ruskin, God's seer." If Emerson may be called the "smile," and Carlyle the "frown," of the nineteenth century, then Ruskin was the century's face transfigured; for there is something ethereal in nearly every feature of his life and thought.

But in a deeper and more philosophical sense these men belong together, for they supplement and complete one another. Plato laid emphasis upon three supreme ideas in the human reason — the ideas of truth, of goodness, and of beauty. And philosophers to-day sometimes inform us that all the higher interests of life may be grouped under the head of what is either true, or good, or beautiful. Carlyle was the impetuous apostle in the last century of what is True. He was forever crying out against all shams and falsities. Emerson, on the other hand, was the great disciple of what is Good. He spoke of the "Sovereignty of Ethics." It was the mission of his life to show that the law of gravity is one with purity of heart and unselfishness of life. John Ruskin, however, was the supreme interpreter of Beauty. His faith was centred in the deep conviction, which he gave his matchless powers to unfold, that the knowledge of what is beautiful is the true path and the first step toward the knowledge of the things which are true and good; and "that the laws of beauty in the material world of God are as eternal and as sacred as, in the world of spirit, virtue is, and, in the world of intelligence, praise."

To many people, however, Ruskin is only a name for oddities, whimsicalities, and eccentricities of life. When the practical man of affairs takes thought of him, there comes the superficial knowledge that he was opposed to railroads, and to most of our modern improvements that come under the head of machinery. The tourist thinks of him — for he is met beneath the shadow of many a great cathedral of Europe and in the presence of the greatest pictures — as a critic of architects and artists. The lover of literature cares only for the sweep and glory of his sentences, and passes by the deep ideas they clothe. The student of political economy is only dimly aware that he gave expression to unorthodox ideas upon trade, and commerce, and the laws of wealth. And of the actual Ruskin, who underlies these superficial and often erroneous ideas, and whose influence is of mighty potency, not only in the world of art but in the world of social reform, no one even yet can speak the final word. But whatever else is vague, uncertain, or matter of dispute, it has to be agreed that Ruskin all his life was preëminently a preacher. A prophet, he had a dream; and the telling of his dream is one of the most precious legacies of the nineteenth century. His mother early dedicated him in her spirit to the Church; and his father, years after he had acquired fame in other lines, used to say regretfully, "He might have been a bishop." He wrote a book upon the *Stones of Venice;* but in every stone of that famous city he found a sermon which taught a lesson for the building of the grander city of the human soul. He lighted for the world of art and literature the *Seven Lamps of Architecture;* but every separate lamp sheds radiant light upon the path of duty. He early made it his mission to study the laws of art. But the laws of art, he soon discovered, were dependent upon the laws of life. He approached the mystery of the world through the gateway of the beautiful, and he soon became aware that beauty was intensely one with duty. He found that if the art of a nation is to be right and its taste refined, the life of the nation must first of all be right. And so, from being an art reformer he came to be a social reformer. As first he had pleaded for the construction of more beautiful buildings, so later he came to plead, with all his fervid eloquence, for the building of a new industrial system. "He seems to me," said Carlyle, "to have the best talent for preaching of all men now alive." And, as later I shall ask you to acknowledge, he had that other talent, too, which preachers are sometimes said to lack — he had an even greater talent for practising the things he preached.

Ruskin began life as a Dissenter of the narrow and evangelical type. His mother was intensely orthodox. She made the boy read the Bible through from cover to cover every year, and she had him learn long passages by heart. To this early training the man in later years attributed his love of literature, and the cultivation of his style in writing; and this is why his books all teem with the aptest and most beautiful interpretations of passages from Scripture. But, as happened so often, and is happening still, when once he overstepped the limits of his early faith, he wandered far afield in the dreary realms of painful doubt. His revolt all dated from a Sunday visit that he paid to a little Protestant chapel at Turin. He found the preacher consigning all the outside world to complete perdition, and promising salvation to the little handful of worshippers who sat before him. The falsity and folly of all such beliefs dawned suddenly upon his mind. It was only gradually that he worked his way upward through his doubts until he reached a larger faith, and firmer. "Of all the saints," he once could say, "I have the deepest sympathy with Saint Thomas. I would fain put all his questions over again, and twice as many more." At one time he even planned to reprint his earlier books with all their religious teachings omitted. But two things saved him from this wilderness of doubt, and made a grander faith his own — his overmastering sense of the glories of nature, and his burning desire to lighten human suffering and woe. A worshipper of nature in all its varied forms, he reached through nature up to nature's God. He came to look on God as the artist of the universe, who is forever working to make man's dwelling place more beautiful; and he could think of Him as the unseen painter who clothes the simple flower of the field with glory far surpassing Solomon's. "I hold the hills and vales of my native land," he could write, "to be the true temples of God, and their waves and clouds holier than the dew of the baptistry and the incense of the altar." The marvels of the outward world were "altars built not to, but by, an Unknown God." We owe it to him, much more than to any other man, if we understand more deeply now than ever, how "the heavens declare the glory of God, and the firmament showeth his handiwork." For Ruskin saw and described the glories of the sky and clouds as no other ever has. But, in addition to the glories of nature, he saw and understood the glories of human nature. He was one with Channing in standing as a champion for the essential dignity of man. "All the sin of men," he said, "I esteem as their disease, and not their nature. And my wonder, even when things are at their worst, is always at the height which this human nature can attain. Thinking it high, I always find it a higher thing than I thought it. When the captain of a ship shakes hands with his mate, saying, 'God speed you: I will go down with my passengers,' that I believe to be human nature."

It was only natural, therefore, that Ruskin gradually left his doubts behind him. He daily grew more sure that "there is a true church wherever one hand meets another helpfully, and that this is the only holy, or mother church, which ever was, or ever shall be." He came to see that "the only constant form of pure religion is in useful work, and faithful love, and stintless charity."

It is fitting, however, that we say something of his life. For what a life it was, when we look at it in fairness, — when we brush aside his eccentricities, his prejudices, his faults of judgment and of temper! The prophet had a dream; and how grandly he told that dream in the utterances of his life! He had his faults, of course; and he needed no one to remind him of them. He was egotistical; he was immoderate in blame as he also was in praise; he let his prejudices warp his judgment often; and he lacked, in some degree, the robuster virtues of life, so that a tinge of the feminine is often apparent in his writings. But to let such failings blind us to his beneficent services for art and humanity is foolish. One recalls the witty advice of Augustine Birrell in regard to Carlyle, who also had — well, let us say, his foibles: "Brother dunces, hold down your heads that I may whisper in your long-furred ears; we do not all have genius, and we can't afford to quarrel with it."

His life would perhaps have been completer had he not shut himself off so resolutely from the world of practical affairs, losing himself in the realm of the ideal. A friend met him once in Florence, just after the news had come of the Soudan, and the fall of the heroic Gordon; and the busy dreamer asks, "But, yes, only who is the Soudan?" While among the Alps, he hears of the death of a favorite cousin; and at once he loses thought of all family difficulties in trying to reproduce the effects of a sunrise. And such may have been in part the secret of his marriage tragedy. Amid his visions and enthusiasms he had almost forgotten that he had a wife, having reverently set her as an idol in a solitary niche, until one day he found that she had fallen in love with his friend, the artist Millais; and the joy of his life died out, and was never to return. Silently he watched her find her happiness with another; and, wretched in his grief, he set himself to relieve the wretchedness of others wherever he might see it.

Ruskin passed through a long and serious crisis in his religious life; but the crisis of his moral life was deeper, more painful, and was fraught with tragedy and pathos. There are those who speak about his "two lives." Till he was forty years old he lived for art. After that, so long as he had strength and thought for anything, he gave himself to humanity. And yet his life in another and a deeper sense was a very grand and simple whole. He was a socialist second, because he was an artist first. And he was both socialist and artist because his long life through he was an ardent worshipper of the beautiful and the good in everything, and a wholesome hater of the ugly and the base wherever found.

John Ruskin was of Scotch descent, and like most Scotsmen he never forgot the fact. His father was a wine merchant—an "entirely honest merchant," the son wrote about him when he died, and considered that the highest possible of tributes. This "honest merchant" had acquired slowly and with pains a fortune of nearly a million dollars. This fortune Ruskin inherited. In the meantime his books had brought him fame. Society opened her doors to the brilliant author. Aristocracy was ready to flatter and to worship him. He had built himself a lordly pleasure house of culture and opportunity. But all this he suddenly sacrificed, cast to the winds, and turned his back upon, courting unpopularity rather than society, misunderstanding rather than flattery, and agonizing work rather than artistic ease. How did this come about? What did it mean? To what lengths did his self-sacrifice lead him?

Ruskin by endeavoring to reform art was brought face to face with the actual conditions of life; and he came to see, or to believe, that if the art of a people were to be improved, the life of the people must first be improved. His sensitive soul was stung into agony by a consciousness of the degraded and wretched conditions under which a large proportion of the people were obliged to live. Industry without art, he felt, was brutality, and the first thing necessary was to change the conditions of industrial life. But the age was selfish. Its spirit was commercial. Competition was its watchword. Material gain was the one thing thought of. The valleys of England were becoming filled with factories. Its hills were hollowed to find coal. The blue of its heaven was blackened by smoke. Its limpid lakes were rimmed with railways. What chance for art, he cried out in despair, when these things are considered signs of a progressive civilization! It seemed to him that the God whom people really worshipped was one who led them indeed as "a pillar of cloud by day and a pillar of fire by night," the cloud being the black smoke of factory chimneys, and the fire the red glare of their furnaces. "This is your God, O ye English," he cried, "and in worshipping him you are making a wilderness of once 'Merrie England,' and ye call it a Paradise because some few of you are growing rich."

In order to understand such passionate words as these we must remember that they were written at the blackest period of English industrial life. The factory system had recently been introduced, and conditions seemed desperate. Our modern sanitary legislation had not grown up. Small attention was paid to human life. Little children were employed in poorly built mills for sixteen, seventeen, eighteen hours a day, and were chained to heavy cars in dismal mines, where they sometimes died of sheer exhaustion. The inhumanity of it all aroused the poetic genius of Mrs. Browning, who wrote her famous plaint of the children; and it stirred the sensitive, beauty-loving Ruskin to the depths of his ardent nature. "The great cry," he declared, "that rises from all our manufacturing cities, louder than their furnace blast, is all in very deed for this — that we manufacture everything there except men; we bleach cotton and strengthen steel, and refine sugar, and shape pottery; but to brighten, to strengthen, to refine, or to form a single living spirit never enters into our estimate of advantages."

The old legend tells us that the Buddha left the luxuries of his palace one silent night, and devoted himself to a wandering life of poverty, that he might discover a way of release from suffering for his fellow men. So this modern reformer left the palace of his wealth, his popularity, his art studies, in order to free his fellow men from the bondage of brutal toil and poverty. His eager desire to be of use laid merciless hold upon him, and haunted him whenever he tried to paint and read and study architecture. He wrote from Venice: "Here is a little gray cockle-shell lying beside me, which I gathered the other evening out of the dust of the Island of St. Helena, and a bright colored snail-shell from the thirsty sands of Lido; and I want to set myself to draw these and describe them in peace. Yes; and all my friends say that is my business. Why can't I mind it, and be happy? . . . But, alas! my prudent friends, little enough of all I have a mind to do may be permitted me; for this green tide which eddies by my threshold is full of floating corpses, and I must leave my dinner and bury them, since I cannot save, and put my cockle-shell in my cap and take my staff in hand to seek an unencumbered shore."

Let us ask where the staff of his passionate desire led him, and where he found the "unencumbered shore" toward which he bent his steps in middle manhood.

The central object of all Ruskin's social teachings was directed against the spirit of "commercialism." It was clear that the main drift of society, under the influence of great industrial innovations, was toward materialism. The "chief end of man," more than in any former age, was to get rich, and this mania for riches trampled many into such depths of poverty as had never before existed. It appeared, therefore, that to lighten the pressure of poverty, society must first be diverted from its passion of material prosperity. The diverting aim must be a love for beauty, and the beautiful was dependent on the good. Did people really appreciate and love the beautiful, they would see that real happiness could not be refined in any furnace or woven on any whirling looms. "Commercialism must be replaced and overcome by a love of the beautiful."

In order, however, really to understand the force of Ruskin's specific theories, we ought properly, first of all, to get a distinct understanding of the theories which he attacked. For his work was in large part controversial, — as every man's must be who does not fight as one who beats the air.

These theories — I refer to them with the greatest possible brevity — were based entirely upon what was called an "economic man." This creature had only one object in existence, namely, to reap the greatest possible amount of material reward with the least possible amount of physical exertion. The one God, in whose hands was the salvation of the entire human race, had revealed Himself upon the Mount of Capital, and was the God of Competition. All wages were regulated by the iron law of "Supply and Demand." Such terms as a "fair" wage or a "living" wage had literally no possible meaning.

Finally, *laissez faire*, "let things alone," was the central article of this selfish creed. All interferences by the State on the ground of justice, or duty, were harmful, and kept society from reaching the millennium.

Such was the gospel of Individualism, utterly divorcing ethics and economics. It was the gospel according to Adam Smith and Stuart Mill, according to Malthus and Ricardo, and according to the manufacturer who worked little children eighteen hours a day in ill-built factories. And it was this gospel which John Ruskin began to denounce, declaring it an unmitigated curse, destroying men's bodies and damning their very souls. Far from leading to any millennium, it was a short cut to perdition, as the growing degradation of the laboring classes bore eloquent testimony. It was of little consequence to him if there was a hell in another life, for the mass of working people had found hell here, where they were overworked like animals and underpaid like slaves. As for the Capitalists, they had but one object, and the worst of it was that in seeking that object they posed as benefactors to the human race. If it should be discovered, he said, that a railway could be built to hell, and become a paying investment, all the stock would be subscribed for in London alone, and that, too, in a single season.

But these "damnatory clauses," if we may use the expression of another, were only typical of the Prophet in his moments of excitement, and they accomplished little except to awaken anger and distrust in others. We may wisely pass them by to look at the wisdom and mercy of his actions, which speak a different language and awaken other feelings which are active still. Let me ask you to take notice of simple facts — not of what he thought, but of what he did; not of what he preached, but of what he practised; not of his books, but of his acts.

Ruskin's father, as we saw, had left him a fortune of nearly a million dollars. This fortune he proceeded systematically and steadily to give away. Refusing to spend the income on himself, he used both principal and income to relieve suffering and establish institutions of reform. For many years he practically supported Rossetti and his wife, buying their pictures and sending themselves away for study or for rest. It seemed to him that the city of Sheffield needed something to encourage artistic ideas in the minds of its iron and steel workers. So he presented the city with a museum of art, which he furnished entirely at his own expense. He did substantially the same for Oxford. He gave the University a school of design, with a collection of rare and priceless works of art; and he endowed the school with $50,000. In the meantime gifts were constantly being made to friends and acquaintances and relatives. To the poor people who lived around him he was a steady benefactor, while he paid his servants what he thought they needed, and supported in their old age the servants of his childhood. As someone

JOHN RUSKIN

has very truly said, "This man counted his treasures as a trust fund, held in the interests of suffering merit or youth's dream and talent. That he was on the London committee for the victualling of Paris in 1871 proves that his benevolence was as well known as Mr. Peabody's or Lady Burdett-Coutts's. Taxing himself first a tenth, then half, he finally gave his entire income. If he needed botanical and art works for his studies, he crippled himself rather than refuse his last spare 20 guineas to the widow of a dead artist. If for health's sake, or art's sake, he wanted to take a trip to Switzerland, he would forego it, that he might contribute 100 pounds to the Cruikshank memorial. Riches means money valiantly used, and he saw to it, therefore, that his wealth was invested in men. He felt that money put into young men would go farther than in stone walls. He sought out young artists and bade them paint for him; young authors, and bade them write for him; sweet singers, and bade them sing for him; young reformers, and bade them speak for him, pray for him. 'Mr. Ruskin and Lord Shaftesbury have held the working people of Great Britain back from hopelessness,' saith the great labor leader. The influence of this single personality in times of social strife and unrest has wrought more effectually against anarchy and social chaos than whole battalions of policemen."

But of greater consequence than the size of the gifts were the discernment and purpose with which they were given. Ruskin's name will always be associated with some of the most approved and widespread methods of philanthropy. Every charity worker in America, as in England, is familiar, for instance, with the name of Octavia Hill. But Octavia Hill was Ruskin's agent. In order to test certain of his theories, he bought a tract of miserable tenements in one of the wretchedest parts of London. Such property generally yielded its owners anywhere from ten to twenty per cent. But Ruskin put the houses into the hands of Miss Hill, asking her to collect the rents, improve the buildings, and reform the tenants, suggesting that five per cent. was all the return he wished. The undertaking laid the foundation of certain modern methods of "associated charity."

Scarcely less intimate was Ruskin's connection with the scheme of a University Settlement. He had written once, "I tell you that neither sound art, policy, nor religion can exist in England until, neglecting if need be your own pleasure-gardens and pleasure-chambers, you resolve that the streets, which are the habitations of the poor, shall be again restored to the rule of the Spirit." Some such words as these he spoke once to a body of students in his rooms at Oxford. Arnold Toynbee was one of those pupils, and Toynbee straightway left the pleasure-garden of his life for the poverty of London streets. And the residents of Toynbee Hall to-day, the first of the University Settlements, look back to Ruskin as the spiritual father of that noble work.

In the meantime, he gave a large part of what remained to him of his fortune to establish a "country colony," where the wretched poor of the city might be given healthy work, and encouraged toward a new start in life. "We will try," he declared, "to make some small piece of English ground beautiful, peaceful, and fruitful. We will have no untended and unthought-of creatures on it. None wretched but the sick, none idle but the dead."

And so at last his wealth was all distributed; and nothing was left him to live on but the returns from his books, which, however, more than covered all his needs. In the Armenian Convent of St. Lazzaro near Venice I remember seeing an autograph letter from Ruskin written several years ago. It has been framed and hangs upon a wall. He had been appealed to for funds in order that a part of the Convent which had been destroyed by fire might be rebuilt. And what did he answer? This: "*I long ago gave away all my fortune thinking to be dead before now;* but I will send what I can." In his own lifetime he had not only made, but executed, his will; and his bequests were so boundless for that day that the conservative representatives of the English aristocracy cried out in alarm that his example would undermine the foundations of society.

But greater — infinitely greater — than the simple sacrifice of his wealth, which seems to have been a joy, was the sacrifice of ease, and quiet, and peace of mind, and popularity, and social distinction, and well-deserved fame! He had to fight his way against what is worse by far than opposition, namely, ridicule. And yet, in the strength of all his middle-life he would scarcely ever spare himself; and, whenever he lectured upon art, he drove home upon his hearers some fundamental moral or industrial truth. It became almost literally true, as he wrote of himself, "that he could neither paint, nor read, nor look at minerals, nor do anything else he liked, and the very light of the morning sky became hateful to him because of the human misery he was eager to abate." And, that he succeeded in his painful efforts, at least to a very considerable extent, there can be no shadow of doubt.

Ruskin's chief service consisted, however, not so much in what he achieved as in what he suggested. Suggestiveness is the silver thread which flashes out through the varied patterns of his many writings. A single sentence, a phrase, perhaps, will contain a whole philosophy, and light up the dark-

JOHN RUSKIN

ness of many a mystery in life! And so of his social theories and his eager efforts for practical reform. It is not what they are, but to what they point, that makes them significant. Ruskin was forty years before his time in urging combination, or coöperation, as a substitute for competition, and in preaching the benefit of State Control. In 1863 he urged the establishment of a Government Parcels Post, which soon came to be established in England, and after fifty years, or more, was introduced into America. He advocated People's Palaces fifteen years before Walter Besant's book on *All Sorts and Conditions of Men* led to the establishment of the first one; and he was a vehement advocate of municipal art galleries at a time when municipalities had not begun to own even street railways and lighting plants.

The "Arts and Crafts" movement is thoroughly domesticated now. It was inaugurated in large part through the energies of William Morris — the famous designer of chintzes and easy chairs. But really, toward the movement which Morris headed, the way, as usual, had been pointed out by the "far-ranging genius of Ruskin. The Prophet in this case was only some ten years before his age." Nor is it different with the cause of Manual Training, which is now so well established in our public schools. A few years ago a Professor of Pedagogy in Harvard University told me that he would not be satisfied until such schools as Milton Academy and St. Mark's, as Middlesex and Hackley, took their boys out into the fields and taught them to plough and plant, as carefully as they teach them to pitch a ball and to kick a goal. I quoted the remark to the head master of a large boys' school a few years ago, and he was quite derisive on the subject. Yet the Harvard professor had Ruskin's authority to fall back upon, for this is what we read in the *Political Economy of Art*, which was written in the dark ages of 1857: "I believe that all youths, of whatever rank, ought to learn some manual trade thoroughly; for it is quite wonderful how much a man's views of life are cleared by the attainment of the capacity of doing any one thing well with his hands and arms. At this day, the most useful things which boys learn at public schools are, I believe, riding, rowing and cricketing. But it would be far better that members of Parliament should be able to plough straight and make a horseshoe, than only to feather oars neatly, or point their toes prettily in stirrups."

There we have the whole philosophy of manual training in a nutshell. And much the same is true as regards the deeper and more theoretical teachings of this social prophet. Most of those teachings are contained, in embryo, at least, in a little slip of a volume called *Unto this Last*. The chapters which compose the book were to constitute a series of articles in the *Cornhill Magazine*. But, after the second one appeared, the public raised such a hue and cry that Thackeray, who was the *Cornhill* editor at the time, had to decline any further contributions of the kind. The book appeared in due season, however, in a small edition of one thousand copies. Ten years later the edition had not been exhausted. For the past fifty years, however, that book has been selling at the rate of two thousand copies a year, thus justifying Ruskin's own contention that it was the best of his books. It has been translated into French, German, and Italian, and the sale continues still. What the public spurned and cast out as dangerous heresy a half-century ago, it has finally come around to, and is striving to embody in the social order. England, in other words, as someone has well said, — and we now must add America as well, — "is travelling straight, and is moving fast, at the present time, in the direction of Ruskin's most characteristic teaching. Much that he taught, translated into modern English, is but the principle of the minimum wage, the old-age pension, improved housing, and compensation for improvements," although I incline to believe that the author of *Queen's Gardens* and *The Crown of Wild Olive* would have sacrificed all else rather than see the vote conferred on woman.

"The glory of men," declared Wendell Phillips once, "is not what they actually produce, so much as what they enable others to do. My Lord Bacon, as he takes his proud march down the centuries, may lay one hand on the telegraph, and the other on the steamboat, and say, 'These are mine! for I taught you to invent.' And the Puritan, wherever he finds a free altar, free lips, aye, and a free family, may say, 'These are mine!' No matter for the stain of bigotry which rests upon his memory, since he taught us these." And so Ruskin, if he looks down upon our University Settlements and our model tenements and our country colonies, and on our new Political Economy, may say in justice, "These came from me."

In the preface of one of his most beautiful books, *Sesame and Lilies*, he tells us that only two faults in life are of vital consequence — idleness and cruelty. "God," he says, "dislikes idle and cruel people more than any others." His first order is, "Work while you have life," and his second, "Be merciful while you have mercy." And these two orders be certainly obeyed. He worked his eager and excited brain until the light of his reason for a time was clouded, and he carried his mercy to such lengths that people called it weakness. Because he passed "his life in almsgiving, not in fortune hunting; because he labored always for the honor of others, not his own, and chose rather to make men look at Turner and Luini than to form or exhibit the skill of his own hand; because he lowered his rents and assured the comfort of his poor tenants instead of taking from them all he could force for the roofs they needed; because he loved a wood walk better than a London street, and would rather watch a sea-gull fly than shoot it, and rather hear a thrush sing than eat it; finally, because he honored all women with solemn worship, and was kind even to the unthankful and the evil," therefore his critics have been inclined to emphasize "the effeminate sentimentality of Ruskin." But the probability is that it will not be thus in the indefinite future. Time, with kindly touch, will smooth away his foibles; and, as we come to understand the greatness of his soul and the power of his prophecy, we shall gladly put him side by side with Emerson and Carlyle. More and more we shall come to honor the man who, in spite of tragic experience, never lost his faith in woman's purity, and power to influence and guide; more and more as we grow dissatisfied with the sordid and materialistic marriages of our day, and perceive the evils of increasing divorce, we shall value the pure idealism of his *Sesame and Lilies*, with those glowing pages upon "King's Treasuries," and "Queen's Gardens," and "The Mystery of Life." And when, in our national life, we have found the fruit of the "commercial spirit" only dead-sea fruit, and have tasted its bitter ashes, we shall remember the man who tried to teach the world "that there is no wealth but life," and that "that country is the richest which nourishes the greatest number of happy and noble human beings."

The prophet had his dream! Then let us do him reverence for it, and for the glorious way in which he told it to the world. "His words have been carved on marble for a thousand years." He once described Carlyle as one who had been "born in the clouds and struck by the lightning." But the description was truer even of himself than it was of the Chelsea prophet.

There have been few men whose lips have been touched as his were with sacred fire. He had eyes that saw behind the veil, and ears that caught the whisper of heavenly voices. In his vision of the Beautiful, he was met and mastered by a dream of Duty. And the new vision mingled with the old. But he was faithful to them both, and long before death touched him he had found the crown of life.

THE HISTORIAN AS PREACHER

THE HISTORIAN AS PREACHER [1]

WE have had abundant evidence of late, if evidence were needed in the matter, that preaching is not of necessity confined to pulpits, nor a matter solely of the churches of the world. There are sermons which come from men of letters as well as ministers, and from politicians who are genuine prophets. Whatever may be thought about the character of the sermons he delivered, and the nature of the texts from which he drew his inspiration, there can be no question of the fact that Theodore Roosevelt was essentially a preacher. His messages to Congress, which came with more than ministerial regularity and frequency, were essentially homiletical in form as well as hortatory in purpose, and his public addresses might well be collected under the Newmanesque title of *Political and Plain Sermons*.

In all of this there is nothing remarkable, unless it be in the fact that the individual chances to be a statesman and politician, instead of a poet, or a man of letters pure and simple. Most of us remember the question that Coleridge once put to his friend Charles Lamb, and the witty answer

[1] From the *Harvard Theological Review*.

which he instantly received; but perhaps the repetition of it may be pardoned for the sake of those who have forgotten. "Charles," said the poet to his friend, referring to the days when he had been the minister of a Unitarian congregation, — "Charles, did you ever hear me preach?" "I never heard you do anything else," was the ready although stuttering reply. The same might equally well be said of many another person who has either changed his profession or chosen from the first a wholly different calling. The man of letters, for example, is frequently a preacher. Carlyle was, who thundered and sent forth vivid lightnings against every form of folly and abuse that came beneath his eye. Abundant proof that the art critic and reformer often falls into the preaching habit is given by Ruskin, who found a sermon in each stone of Venice, and a text in every letter of its long decay. The man of science indulges often in the art, and does it well, as Thomas Huxley made distinctly clear. Those of us who have visited the Wiertz Museum in Brussels, or remember Verestchagin's exhibition of his pictures showing forth the horrors and barbarities of war, will be ready to confess that the artist also may be numbered in this class. And if men of letters, statesmen, scientists, and artists, with reformers generally, engage at times in a practice which is more especially the privilege of the minister and a func-

THE HISTORIAN AS PREACHER

tion of the church, the same right may be broadly granted to one who has a clearer title to it than any of the others, and better reason for doing it both earnestly and well. I refer to the Historian. In one sense it almost may be said that the historian is always preaching. He may not be aware of it himself, and he may endeavor to refrain from doing so; but the very facts which he marshals in his mind and sets down in his volumes insist on preaching for themselves. They prophesy above his head and without his leave. "History," as Dionysius long ago declared, "is philosophy teaching by example." It is hardly necessary to add that history is helped in this direction in some instances much more than in others, and, whether consciously or not, is often used to prove a point or illustrate some truth.

However all of this may be, I venture to call attention to a case in point where it was done with singular felicity and forcefulness, but with a generous freedom which has caused much misconception. There is perhaps no instance in modern times where the historian was at once so consummate and so constant, so brilliant and so bold a preacher as was Mr. Froude. In this fact alone, I think, or at any rate in this fact chiefly, we discover the reason why he was often accused of carelessness and prejudice, and was attacked for what he declared that history taught. But before

I go on to illustrate from his works themselves this homiletical or pulpit tendency, I wish to call attention to certain manifest and external features in the life and experience of Froude which serve upon the face of things to justify the point of view which I suggest.

There is reason enough to speak of Froude as a preacher when we remember that he belonged to a family of churchmen, and even began life by "taking orders" himself. His father was rector of the church at Dartington in Devonshire and archdeacon of Totnes. He was a character in his way, this proud archdeacon, with a reputation of his own for clerical ability and worldly power. He combined in his person the authority of the churchman and the influence of the local magistrate and landholder, administering his church affairs on one day, and riding to hounds the next, the best-mounted man in the field. He was a living prototype of Trollope's well-known character, Archdeacon Grantley, in the "clerical series." Indeed, it almost seems that Trollope must have had in mind this Devon churchman when he drew the familiar portrait which stands out with such distinctness on the pages of *The Warden* and *Barchester Towers* and *The Last Chronicle of Barset*.

More important than the father, however, so far as early influence, lasting impression, and a guiding stimulus were concerned, was an elder

THE HISTORIAN AS PREACHER

brother — the brilliant, the magnetic, the domineering, the conservative, the ascetic Hurrell Froude, who, though he died at thirty-three, left a deep mark upon the life and thought of the Church of England. Hurrell was the natural mentor of the youngest son of a large and memorable family, and he did not hesitate to make the fullest and completest use of the power which naturally belongs to an older brother. Moreover, the men who were his friends, and who became associated with him in the Oxford movement, were not without their influence. It was a very remarkable group which was gathered often at the rectory in Dartington, and the boy of twelve or fifteen years listened eagerly to the talk of Newman and Keble when they spent their holidays with his brother. The intimacy was close and confidential. Newman especially was a welcome visitor at the rectory, and he told the world in his *Letters and Correspondence* how one of his *Parochial and Plain Sermons*, entitled "Scripture a Record of Human Sorrow," was suggested by the sight of blooming youth and high spirits in the Froude household, which affected him suddenly with the thought of what changes and what hard discipline and trials were inevitably in store.

When Anthony Froude went up to Oxford, therefore, he was naturally brought into close and very friendly touch with Newman. The influence of that great ecclesiastic could not fail to be distinct as well as deep. Froude followed naturally, though not without misgivings, the career marked out for him. Elected Fellow of Exeter College after graduation, he took deacon's orders, as was then required of all Fellows, and he preached his first and only sermon proper in St. Mary's Church at Babbacombe, a few miles from his home at Dartington. Of the break that later came, of the abandonment of the clerical career, of the loss of belief, of the growth of heretical opinions and the publication of the *Nemesis of Faith*, a copy of which was publicly burned in the Hall of Exeter College, and of how he finally came to devote himself to history — of things like these we need not speak.

I have called attention to these scanty biographical details not only for the purpose of showing that Froude was from the first trained to be a preacher, but because the things he came in the end to preach through the medium of history were the very opposite of those which it was hoped that he would set forth as a churchman. In a rash and over-confident moment Hurrell Froude had told his younger brother that when Newman and Keble disagreed, then, but not till then, he might do his thinking for himself. What seemed to the young enthusiast utterly impossible in regard to his two most intimate friends was very soon to come to pass. To the astonishment and conster-

THE HISTORIAN AS PREACHER

nation of his followers and friends, Newman in 1845 slipped quietly into the Church of Rome, leaving Keble and the rest to pursue their way as rigid Church of England men. Before the unexpected actually came to pass, Anthony Froude had begun to claim his rights of independent thought, and, as often happens, there came about a strong reaction from the narrow tenets which had been impressed upon his mind. It was said of Macaulay that he wrote "his History to prove that God was always on the side of the Whigs." With an equal amount of truth, or untruth, it may be said that Froude wrote his glowing and dramatic History to prove that God was on the side of the Protestants.

The strength of his convictions, or, if you please, the vehemence of his prejudice, upon this point, is largely to be accounted for by the way in which his beliefs took hold upon his mind. He had been trained to hold the very opposite position. To his elder brother and his friends the Protestant Reformation, as it came to be worked out in England under Henry VIII, was a terrible and almost fatal error. They had no sympathy with the Puritan, none with the English martyrs in the time of Mary. "I am glad to know something of the Puritans," wrote Hurrell Froude to Keble upon one occasion, "as it gives me a greater right to hate Milton, and accounts for many of the things which disgusted me in his, not-in-my-sense-of-the-word, poetry. Also," he added, "I adore King Charles and Bishop Laud."

It was in such an atmosphere that the future author of *The History of England from the Fall of Wolsey to the Defeat of the Spanish Armada* was reared. When he began to think for himself, and read for himself, and finally to study and gather facts for himself, it was no wonder that he underwent a fierce reaction. What he came to see appeared all the more glorious and important, because he had worked his way onward toward it not without difficulty and not without pain and grievous misunderstandings and opposition. In dramatic contradiction, therefore, to what he had been brought up to believe, and had been urged by family and friends to preach in the pulpit, he set himself to proclaim in his History not the shame, but the endless glory, of the English Reformation; not the reasons for hating, but those for adoring, the Puritan; not the causes for believing that Henry VIII and Latimer and Cranmer were individuals to be reprobated and repented of, while Charles I and Laud were loved; but the very opposite of this — namely, that Henry and his followers were the champions of English liberty and the actual saviours of the country. With the unerring eye of genius he chose for his theme the mighty drama when Protestant England under Henry and

THE HISTORIAN AS PREACHER

Elizabeth was clutched in a death-struggle with the Catholic forces, and from first to last we see the superior qualities of those who held to the Reformation position in religion. In the fight that goes on, the God of battles is on the side of the greater honesty and fervor of the Protestants and their devotion to truth and freedom. Froude himself has declared that Macaulay's unfairness to Cranmer, in the celebrated review of Hallam's Constitutional History, first suggested to him the project of his work. It was thus for the purpose of contradicting falsehood, of setting the past in a truer light before his countrymen, and of saving them from the errors in which he had himself been trained, that he set to work.

Having chosen his theme and gathered with abundant pains and care a mass of original material, Froude claimed the right, which lately has been too often neglected, — partly perhaps because the spell of science rests upon our age, and partly because in large measure the power itself has been lost, — he claimed the right to make history interesting, and he believed that it was none the less true when interpreted and written as a drama. He called to his assistance the one great thing which he had gained of Newman and the Oriel atmosphere — a matchless style which never failed him, and which enabled him, as one of his fiercest and unfairest critics has confessed, when he came to certain central episodes, such as the sinking of Spain's great Armada, to rise "into a species of epic power."

"History and story," it has well been said, "are variations of the same word, and the historian who is a master of his art must be a storyteller." In this respect Froude was well calculated to meet the requirements of the "Gentle Reader," who claimed that history should be readable, and who described his feelings when he was set adrift on one of those bottomless seas of erudition called history, without human companionship, and only "writings, writings everywhere and not a page to read." The simple fact of the matter is that Froude did not write his histories merely to be referred to; he wrote them to be read. He did not design them to stand upon dusty bookshelves, but he prepared them for the hands of living men and women who wished to know about the past. To him the presentation of facts was almost as important as the facts themselves. And in this he was essentially Greek, — a lover of art as well as science, of beauty as well as accuracy. He was interested in history because of what it taught, and he was prejudiced enough to believe that it had many things to teach the coming generations. He was not warned off from his task, nor deterred from doing it well, by the modern claim "that history is a science and not a province of literature;

that the time has not yet come to draw any conclusions or to summarize any tendencies; that picturesque narrative is an offence against the spirit of truth." Far from it. He agreed rather with Professor Seeley, that "we do not so much want history explained after the manner of science as we want it portrayed and interpreted after the manner of literature." He believed, indeed, with a present-day historian of wide repute [1] that "the assembling of details is antiquarian; the truth of general effect alone is historical. To produce the latter is masterly; the former is mechanical investigation, and its reproduction for the laity misleads far more frequently than it guides." It is the business and the privilege of the historian, quite as much as it is the business and privilege of the preacher, to point a moral and adorn a tale; and the moral is not the less sound for being pointed gracefully and well, nor the tale less accurate and faithful for being draped in the adornment of splendid rhetoric and rich description. History is essentially a form of eloquence. It requires imagination; and it cannot make us understand until it makes us *see* things. In this respect Froude was essentially a master, and seldom if ever has he been surpassed in insight and power to depict the past. He belongs to the class of Prescott and of Parkman, of Motley and of Macaulay, men who have "dis-

[1] W. M. Sloane, *Atlantic Monthly*, August, 1908, page 280.

played the romantic side of history, and have discovered the possibilities of language in rendering its records glowing and fascinating without departing from veracity." Nevertheless it was just because Froude knew and used the possibilities of the English language that he came to be so freely and frequently accused of departing from veracity.

Into the question of Froude's reliability, however, I have no wish, nor perhaps am I equipped, to enter. But it ought to be said that since the charges against him have been traced to their turbulent and angry source, the prejudices that once prevailed have tended silently to pass away. According to Sir Edmund Gosse, in his *History of English Literature*,[1] Freeman, who was a firm high-churchman, could never forgive his brilliant rival for abandoning the party in the old Oxford days. He sat at his literary elbow like some gigantic Nemesis for more than thirty years, magnifying every fault, and exaggerating every error in his historical writings, though often falling into gross errors himself in the process. His criticisms for the most part were anonymous, but were always written with rancor and abuse. "Any stick," he once declared, "was good enough with which to belabor Froude." Freeman at his gentlest was never too refined, and at his harshest became insulting. He was introduced in public once as

[1] *A Short History of Modern English Literature*, page 373.

THE HISTORIAN AS PREACHER

"the historian who has done so much to reveal to us the rude manners of our ancestors."

It must not be inferred from this, however, that Froude was free from errors, or beyond the range of criticism. He was a pioneer, and it has been truly said of him that "probably no previous historian has incorporated so much unpublished material in his work."[1] His authorities for the most part were in manuscript. They were written in five languages, and filled nine hundred volumes. The most precious of them were in the little village of Simancas in Spain, which he was the first to explore. He copied masses of documents which even a Spaniard would have found it difficult to read, and these copies were later given to the British Museum, where they may now be seen. I hold no brief for Froude's inerrancy, however, and I would not for a moment claim that he did not make mistakes, it may be serious ones. But I do assert that his errors have been grievously exaggerated, and that the greatest of all historical writers, since history began, have not escaped a similar charge. Carlyle, for instance, was accused of misrepresenting events in the French Revolution, and all of us know how severely Bancroft suffered in the old days. Professor Sloane has called to mind an instance of the ill-deserved censure in the latter case. When New Jersey was

[1] *Dictionary of National Biography*, Supplement, vol. ii, p. 257.

erecting the battle monument at Trenton, and proposed on the authority of Bancroft's pages to inscribe on its base Lord George Germain's terse words about "that unhappy affair which has blasted all our hopes," it was a Boston historian who dryly remarked in a letter that this was "one of the things Bancroft thought ought to have been said, but there was no proof that it ever *was* said." The phrase so calmly dismissed as invention was promptly found by a friendly fellow student of the historian in the pages of Parliamentary debates.

I can give a similar incident in regard to Froude, which will show at once how falsely he was sometimes judged, and how unfairly. Not long ago I was talking with a distinguished historical writer, who is also one of the most careful. The discussion turned on Froude, and he offered to give me an instance of his errors, inaccuracy, and unscrupulous methods. In his sketch of Cæsar, he said, Froude tells us that after the battle of Pharsalia, Cæsar burned all Pompey's letters without reading them, not wishing to learn unpleasant things about his friends at home. "Now that statement," said my friend, "is a very interesting one; but there is absolutely no foundation for it. I have consulted Mommsen, and last year when I was in Rome, I asked some learned men of my acquaintance if they could tell me Froude's authority. They could

THE HISTORIAN AS PREACHER

not, the fact being that he undoubtedly made it up out of whole cloth." As a matter of fact, however, I soon discovered the entire incident, set down as Froude related it, in the pages of Dion Cassius. My friend, to whom I wrote, replied that "one swallow does not make a summer," and that actual instances could probably be found of mistakes that Froude had fallen into. And so no doubt they could. My only contention is that justice never has been done him, and that he was loaded down unfairly from the first with a reputation for carelessness. The judgments, however, that time often renders in respects like these are as interesting as any judgments that are handed down to us in silence, and they often have all the dramatic features of what is anomalous and paradoxical. A good example of what I mean may be found in the case of Herodotus *versus* his detractors. Macaulay, for instance, in his brilliant and interesting essay upon History, did not hesitate to pass the most sweeping judgment on the recognized father of this branch of literature. "At the distance of three and twenty centuries," he wrote, "we feel for him the same sort of pitying fondness which Fontaine and Gay are said to have inspired in society. He has written an incomparable book. He has written something better perhaps than the best history; but he has not written a good history. He is, from the first to the last chapter, an inventor. We do not here refer," he goes on to say, "merely to those gross fictions with which he has been reproached by the critics of later times. We speak of that coloring which is equally diffused over the whole narrative, and which perpetually leaves the most sagacious reader in doubt what to reject and what to receive. The most authentic parts of his work bear the same relation to his wildest legends which Henry V bears to the Tempest."

Thus the great Macaulay on the careless and credulous Herodotus! Very steadily, however, since the words were written, the case has gone against the facile Englishman and in favor of the ancient Greek. Careful study and a wider knowledge of ancient times and people have gone, I believe, to show that much which was tossed aside as fiction in Herodotus was actual fact, while Macaulay's own history has gradually become discredited, because of its partisan judgments and its perpetual inaccuracy.

The fact of the matter is that there are two great kinds of history, and probably there always will be. The writing of history, in short, is not unlike the art of painting. In both great spheres there are distinct and opposing schools. There are the artists who make a science of detail, and there are those who make a science of *impression*, and neither school is ever wholly accurate, nor can it hope to be.

THE HISTORIAN AS PREACHER

Now Froude was emphatically an impressionist and a color-schemist. He painted scenes in a vivid and expressive way, and he loved a dramatic situation. He made the most of a striking episode, and the only difference between himself and other writers lay in the fact that where others failed, or did but fairly well, he set a masterpiece before the reader's mind. Froude may have hated correcting proof, as Mr. Birrell has declared,[1] and he was doubtless careless in the copying of manuscript; but he had a veritable passion for digging into the records of the past, and he never wearied in his task of making real the men and women whom he found there. His History may live to be corrected, and his portraits to become retouched; but at least they are likely to live and to be remembered, which is more than can be said of the writings of many of those who delighted to abuse him.[2]

From this digression, however, which has not been wholly vain if it has removed from our minds some portion of inherited prejudices, let us come back to our proper subject, — the preaching qualities of this historian.

Froude's theme — as we have seen — was the Protestant Reformation and the course it ran in

---

[1] Augustine Birrell, *Essays and Addresses*, page 163.

[2] "It is easy to criticise Froude but hard to improve upon him. His History is the best general survey of the period down to the year 1588." *Mr. Secretary Walsingham and the Policy of Queen Elizabeth*, by Conyers Read, 1926.

England. His text was substantially this, that "the Reformation was the hinge on which all modern history turned." The Reformation, however, as he saw it, was no simple contest between rival creeds and dogmas; it rather was a wide revolt of the laity against the clergy, of the people against a corrupt and tyrannous form of government, of the human mind against restrictions on the native right of independent judgment. As his biographer, Mr. Herbert Paul, reminds us, Froude believed "the Church of Rome to have been the enemy of human freedom under British independence," and in his opinion the "reformers alike in England, in France, and in Germany were fighting for truth, honesty, and private judgment, against priestcraft and ecclesiastical tyranny." He knew too well, from what he had himself been taught, that "the reformers had been calumniated," and it seemed to him that "their services were in danger of being forgotten, and that the modern attempt to ignore the Reformation was not only unhistorical but disingenuous." In this belief he was very far from being alone. Visitors to Oxford will remember the martyrs' monument, opposite Balliol College, near the place where Cranmer, Ridley, and Latimer were burned. The monument, which was designed by Sir G. G. Scott, was erected in 1841, and was intended as a public dissent from the disparagement which

THE HISTORIAN AS PREACHER

had been cast by the leaders of the Oxford movement on the work and influence of the English reformers. It stands there as a witness, raised by scholars and lovers of historical justice, to the worth of men who had laid down their lives in devotion to a mighty cause. What was accomplished there in bronze and marble, Froude undertook to do in literature, and his History is a monument in honor of the martyrs, and likewise of the countless men and women, known and unknown, who bore the brunt of the mighty battle for freedom of thought and national religious independence.

It would be idle to undertake to claim for Froude what he never undertook to claim for himself — an absence of prejudice. "I do not pretend," he wrote long after his History had become a classic, "to be impartial. I believe the Reformation to have been the greatest incident in English history; the root and source of the expansive force which has spread the Anglo-Saxon race over the globe and imprinted the English genius and character on the constitution of mankind." In this respect again he meets in the fullest way the demands of the Gentle Reader. "I have had enough of this," says Mr. Crothers, in his inimitable way, as regards one of our modern scientific historians who has no sympathy and ventures to express no judgments. "I have had enough of this," referring to the Civil War in England. "What I want to know is, what it is all about, and which side on the whole has the right of it. Which side are you on? Are you a Roundhead or a Cavalier? Are your sympathies with the Whigs or the Tories? . . . It's all in confidence; speak out as one gentleman to another under a friendly roof! What do you think about it? No matter if you make a mistake or two, I'll forget most that you say anyway. All that I care for is to get the gist of the matter."

Now that is just what Froude did. He spoke out. He said what he thought, and he gave the gist of the entire matter in graphic and most forceful words. He saw distinctly that the question which was fought out after the fall of Wolsey and finally settled by the defeat of Philip's Great Armada was the question whether England should be bond or free, stagnant or progressive, decadent or resurgent. In the great struggle which ensued before that question was finally settled, men took opposite sides, and took them with a will. Some of the best men of that day, or of any day, took the wrong side, while certain other men whose influence and character never had been rightly weighed, distinctly took the right side. So Froude at least believed. And he not only said so, but he set himself to prove it, and very happily the events of history were on his side. The facts bore out his theory, and the right men and the nobler principles

THE HISTORIAN AS PREACHER

secured the victory which has never since been lost. There can be no doubt that he went too far in acting as the champion of Henry VIII. He would have accomplished more in this direction, as John Fiske well declared, "if he had not tried to do so much." It was a mighty thing, however, to accomplish anything at all; and whether the better and the truer view was suggested to him by Carlyle or not is a matter of very little consequence. The fact remains that what Carlyle himself accomplished in so great a way for Cromwell, his friend and disciple accomplished in a smaller way for a much less noble and attractive character. It was impossible to whitewash Henry completely; but it was much, at least, to set him in a whiter and a clearer light.

We have seen what Froude's text was, and what the general subject of his long discourse. It now remains to consider how he developed and carried through his theme, and what the special truths were that he took delight in emphasizing.

I. Chief among such truths was the value and the surpassing might of vigorous and independent manhood. Like Carlyle, to whom the early volumes of the History were referred for criticism and advice, Froude dearly loved to deal with men, and more especially with men of action — men who did things and engaged in great heroic feats. These were the kind of men which his native

Devonshire had produced in great abundance, and in youth he had been fed upon the tales of what they mightily accomplished. Moreover, he freely accepted the dictum, and worked upon it, that "history is the quintessence of many biographies." He believed that history is essentially a drama and that to be written successfully, it must be written in dramatic fashion. A drama, however, depends upon the movements and positions, the beliefs and undertakings, of its actors. It peoples the stage with living men and actual women. In accomplishing this Froude was assisted by his marvellous imaginative powers. He was possessed of insight; that is, of historical insight. He had the faculty, without which true history never can be written, of living in the age with which he dealt. He touched elbows with the people of past times and succeeded to a wonderful degree in seeing with their eyes and thinking their thoughts. He was with a boatman in his wherry on the Thames that summer afternoon when the "thunder cloud drew down over London, and the storm broke which destroyed St. Paul's." Amidst the roar of the thunder he saw a jagged line of lightning "touch for an instant the highest point of the proud cathedral. Pale tongues of fire flickered out into a coronet of light, and very soon the whole spire, the envy of the Christian world, from the tower wall to the summit, was a gigantic pyramid of flame."

At another time, with three hundred knights and gentlemen, he had been admitted to the hall of Fotheringay Castle to witness the execution of the unfortunate Mary Stuart. He sees her as she descends the great staircase to the hall, leaning on the arm of an officer of the guard. "The tables and forms had been removed," he notices, "and a great wood fire was blazing in the chimney. The Queen of Scots as she swept in seemed as if coming to take part in some solemn pageant. Not a muscle of her face could be seen to quiver. She ascended the scaffold with absolute composure, looked round her smiling, and sat down."

At still another time, he was with the monks in the chapel of the Charterhouse when they prepared themselves with unobtrusive nobleness to die. Not less beautiful "they seemed to him in their resolution, not less deserving the remembrance of mankind, than those three hundred who in the summer morning sat combing their golden hair in the passes of Thermopylæ." He could not "regret their cause, as there *is* no cause for which any man can more nobly suffer than to witness that it is better for him to die than to speak words which he does not mean."

There are those among historians who make it clear that what they care for most is the idle gossip of history, — the trivial events, the passing superstitions, the thoughts and sayings of the stable, the kitchen, and the court. Others, again, and among them the greatest and most searching writers, are interested more especially in social and industrial conditions and the slow development of thought. But Froude, in the first chapter of the first of his twelve long volumes, made it reasonably clear that his chief concern was to be with the sturdy men of his native land and the deeds they sturdily performed in fighting for religious freedom. In this respect he reached a climax when he came to tell the story of the mighty naval duel between Spain and England, in which Drake, and Hawkins, and Sir Walter Raleigh sailed forth to destroy the clumsy but almost countless vessels of the cruel Philip. It was just the kind of theme that suited best the genius of this brilliant descriptive writer, for Froude was a sailor from his youth, and loved the sea as he loved nothing else, unless it were his native Devonshire.

It was not by chance that an older brother made himself one of the foremost naval authorities in England, for the Froudes were a boating family, and the opportunity was near at hand, as the River Dart flowed near the door of the quiet rectory, while the sea was not far off. Even the ritualistic Hurrell could not resist its charm, and he complained in his diary that the thought of it distracted him beyond measure in his prayers. "Do you remember," he wrote Keble, "the south-

THE HISTORIAN AS PREACHER

westerly waves roaring round 'the Prawle' after our stern, and the little crisp breakers that we went through when you cruised with us off Dartmouth harbor?" This passion for the sea, however, was strongest of all with the youngest of the brothers, and he once wrote to a friend that his "highest realization of human felicity would be to wander round the world in a hundred-ton schooner."

With passionate fervor, therefore, as well as intimate knowledge of the elements with which he dealt, he wrote the graphic story of the famous sea fight, and through it all you feel the breezes as they blew across the swaying decks and fanned the cheeks of those mighty men who sailed from Plymouth Harbor to fight the battle of their Queen. It was no wonder that when the story had been told the historian felt that his task was finished. It was the crowning feat of sixteenth-century manhood; or, as he himself expressed it, "It was the sermon which completed the conversion of the English nation and transformed the Catholics into Anglicans."

II. But if Froude believed above all things else in manhood, and preached the need and value of strong and resolute and fearless and liberty-loving men, he also believed in a power that is superior to men and women and orders their affairs. Although his faith in early life had undergone a shock, and, guided by the teachings of Carlyle he lost his hold on dogmatic religion, he never ceased to believe in the presence of a Higher Power which guides men in their work.

"Justice and truth," he once declared, "alone endure and live. Injustice and falsehood may be long-lived; but doomsday comes to them at last, in French Revolutions and other terrible ways." To him there was, if men would only listen, "a Voice forever sounding across the centuries the laws of right and wrong." It came to be his task as an historian to interpret the accents of that voice, and to spell the words it spoke in a mighty human crisis. "Religion," he explained in one connection, — and the words are very strikingly a preacher's words, — "Religion is the attitude of reverence in which noble-minded people instinctively place themselves towards the Unknown Power which made man and his dwelling-place. It is the natural accompaniment of their lives, the sanctification of their actions and their acquirements. It is what gives to man in the midst of the rest of creation his special elevation and dignity. Accompanying our race as it has done from the cradle of civilization, it has grown with our growth, it has expanded with the expansion of knowledge, subject only to the condition that when errors have been incorporated into religious systems, they have been exceptionally tenacious of their ground. Rituals and creeds have become so priceless when once accepted, that it has been held sacrilege to touch them. They have been guarded by superstition and sealed against change by anathema. The eternal nature of the Object of our reverence has been attributed to the forms under which it has been adored, and unable notwithstanding to escape the changes which the development of knowledge imposes upon it, religion has advanced, not by easy and natural transitions, but by successive revolutions, violent leaps, spasmodic and passionate convulsions. Piety, the twin brother of science, tends at such times to be the guardian of error. Love of truth is forced into unnatural hostility with the virtue which is only second to it, and then come those trying periods of human history, when devotion and intelligence appear to be opposed, and the metal of which men and nations are composed is submitted to a crucial test. Those who adhere at all costs to truth, who cling to her though she lead them into the wilderness, find beyond it a promised land where all that they sacrificed is restored to them." [1]

III. As these words suggest, with the emphasis they lay upon the dangerous tenacity of ritual and creed, the religion which Froude believed in and proclaimed was a religion of toleration and kind-

[1] Volume xii, pages 535, 536.

ness. History taught him, and he used the facts of history to proclaim, the dangers of departing from that "pure religion" and undefiled, of trust and love, of reverence and mercy, which was set forth in the gospels. "Such a creed," he declared in one connection, "had it remained as it came from its Founder, would have changed the aspect of the earth. . . . It would not have quarrelled over words and forms. It would have accepted the righteous act whether the doer of it preferred Paul or Cephas. In that Religion hate would have no place, for love, which is hate's opposite, was its principle; nor could any cruel passion have found its sanction where each emotion was required to resolve itself into charity.

"But the rules of life as delivered in the Gospel were too simple and too difficult. . . . God gave the Gospel, the father of lies invented theology. . . . By their fruits ye shall know them. Through Christ came charity and mercy. From theology came strife and hatred, and that fatal root of bitterness which the Lord spoke Himself in the mournful prophecy, that He had not come to send peace on earth, but a sword. When His name and His words had been preached for fifteen centuries, there were none found who could tolerate difference of opinion on the operation of Baptism, or on the nature of His presence in the Eucharist; none, or at least none but the hard hearted chil-

THE HISTORIAN AS PREACHER

dren of the world. The more religious any man was, the more eager was he to put away by fire and sword all those whose convictions differed from his own. The Reformation was the beginning of a new order of things." [1]

Those are biting and sarcastic words; and they are the words of a man whose heart and conscience were aflame with the tragic facts of intolerance and bigotry, and who wished to proclaim these facts from the pulpit page of history.

IV. Again, however, and even more conspicuously, he believed in freedom — freedom of thought, freedom of action, and freedom of religious worship. He believed in the thoroughgoing separation of church and state, and was never tired of laying emphasis upon the obstacles and dangers of every form of ecclesiastical dictation. It is in this connection, much more, so far as I have found, than in any other, that he throws aside all possible disguise and preaches with persistent fervor. There can be no better instances of this than occur in the descriptive passages which tell of the martyrs' deaths at Oxford. What, for instance, could flavor more distinctly of the pulpit than the following: "Latimer was then introduced — eighty years old now — dressed in an old threadbare gown of Bristol frieze, a handkerchief on his head with a night-cap over it,

[1] Volume ix, pages 301, 303.

and over that again another cap, with two broad flaps buttoned under the chin. A leather belt was round his waist, to which a Testament was attached; his spectacles, without a case, hung from his neck. So stood the greatest man perhaps then living in the world, a prisoner on his trial, waiting to be condemned to death by men professing to be the ministers of God. As it was in the day of the prophets, so it was in the Son of man's day; as it was in the days of the Son of man, so was it in the Reformers' day; as it was in the days of the Reformers, so will it be to the end, so long and so far as a class of men are permitted to hold power, who call themselves the commissioned and authoritative teachers of truth." [1]

The same characteristics vividly appear when the death of Cranmer is described. Biblical allusions came almost as easily and naturally to Froude's mind as they came to the mind of Ruskin, and he used them with the preacher's freedom. "So perished Cranmer. He was brought out, with the eyes of his soul blinded, to make sport for his enemies, and in his death he brought upon them a wider destruction than he had effected by his teaching while alive. Had they been contented to accept the recantation, they would have left the Archbishop to die broken-hearted, pointed at by the finger of pitying scorn; and the

[1] Volume vi, page 303.

THE HISTORIAN AS PREACHER

Reformation would have been disgraced in its champion. They were tempted, by an evil spirit of revenge, into an act unsanctioned even by their own bloody laws; and they gave him an opportunity of redeeming his fame, and of writing his name in the roll of martyrs. The worth of a man must be measured by his life, not by his failures under a single and peculiar trial. The Apostle, though forewarned, denied his Master on the first alarm of danger; yet the Master who knew his nature in its strength and its infirmity, chose him for the rock on which He would build His Church." [1]

I could give other instances where, between his graceful periods and sweeping sentences, we catch clear echoes of the pulpit. But I content myself with these.

And so we leave this prince among the men who have aided history in the truths it cannot help but preach. Often hasty in his judgments, mistaken doubtless in certain of his statements, and swayed by prejudices which he took small pains to hide, he none the less was always brilliant, stimulating, and instructive in his treatment of the things concerning which he wrote. It has well been said of him that "Whether for felicity of diction or for vividness of presentation, he belongs indisputably to the company of the Immortals." Because he considered the presentation of facts almost as

[1] Volume vi, pages 429, 430.

important as the facts themselves, and gave in smooth and interesting words the substance of some dull and dry original, it has been assumed of him unfairly that he was careless in his methods and indifferent to "the accidents of truth." But the principle which he laid down for himself at the outset of his work, and the ideal to which he struggled to be true, lacked nothing either in soundness or in height. "It is not," he wrote at the close of the first volume of the History, after clearing the ground for his discourse, "it is not for the historian to balance advantages. His duty is with facts."

THE MYSTICISM OF MAETERLINCK

THE MYSTICISM OF MAETERLINCK[1]

A LITTLE volume of essays by Maurice Maeterlinck caused the author to be proclaimed some thirty years ago with a flourish of French trumpets as the "Belgian Shakespeare," the "European Emerson," and the "greatest mystic of the age." And these epithets and designations were not without some reason. *The Treasure of the Humble*, which helped to call them out, became of genuine soul-value to many people who could lay no claim to that particular virtue. The author's later essays, too, were conceived in a somewhat similar vein. *The Buried Temple* and *The Double Garden* contain hidden teachings of a deep and subtle character, which, being born of spiritual insight, shed light upon the path of destiny and duty.

The fame of Maeterlinck from a purely popular point of view was very limited until his entrancing little play of *The Blue Bird* was put upon the stage. It was the first of the author's many dramas to prove popular — the first perhaps that was clear as to its meaning; one might almost say, the first in which it was possible to know what the author

[1] From the *Harvard Theological Review*.

really meant. He came out at last from the shadows into the sunlight; he forsook the depths of gloomy woods, where the scenes of so many of his previous plays were laid, and gave himself up to interpret the hearts and minds of little children. For this reason, as for many others, it seems worth while to study with some care the teachings of a man whose message might appear to be falling on a deaf, or somewhat heedless, world. In an age of socialism here is a prophet of individual salvation, and at a time when material welfare is the thing considered most, it is refreshing to find someone talking of the soul. And yet, in another way, it may be said that Maeterlinck is one of the most typical teachers that our age contains. He is a startling epitome of the state of modern thought. In him and his teachings we may see what the world apparently is coming to, if not indeed where it actually has arrived.

We can hardly speak of Maeterlinck, however, as a distinctly modern prophet. There is a curious atmosphere of mediævalism about all he writes; a mingling of the old and new, of the ancient East and the modern West. Although he lives in the twentieth century, and finds twentieth-century readers in abundance, there seem to cling about him the garments of the century that nurtured Francis of Assisi, or of that later age which gave birth to a Saint Theresa, or a Madame Guyon.

THE MYSTICISM OF MAETERLINCK

To explain this we must look for a moment at the conditions out of which he came, and consider the environment that helped to shape him with delicate and gentle hands.

Professor Royce has said that William James was distinctly American in his philosophy. In an interesting address before the Harvard Phi Beta Kappa he called attention to the fact that James's pragmatism was an outgrowth of a civilization whose watchword is "efficiency," and that America, and no other country in the world, could have brought to birth and nourished to perfection that free and daring style, with its forceful images drawn from local life and speech. In James, he declared, "certain characteristics of our national life have found their birth. . . . His robust faith is the spirit of the frontiersman, of the gold-seeker, of the home-builder, transferred to the metaphysical and religious realm." And so it is, in a precisely opposite direction, with Maeterlinck. In his books, and the style they are written in, we seem to see a clear and true reflection of the quiet courtyards, the shaded convent gardens, and the bent and gray old gateways leaning for support against some thick-set, moss-grown wall, that are so distinctive of his native land. There are few parts of Europe where the veil of mediævalism lies so closely drawn across the face of things as it does in certain corners of Flanders. It is all the more apparent, moreover, for being violently rent and torn in places by the insistent and intruding hands of modern industry and enterprise. This is true, for instance, of such towns as Bruges and Ghent. Bruges is one of the sleepiest old cities on the continent of Europe. Its dull and stagnant, but winding, picturesque canals appear to find a counterpart in the slow-moving and deliberate currents of traffic and of trade. Nor is Ghent much different from it except in having felt more heavily the great black hand of modern factory life — a hand of death indeed to the beautiful, the artistic, and the picturesque. In Ghent, therefore, to a singular extent the new and old stand forth as deadly rivals, while the mediæval and the modern jostle one another openly upon the streets. Many a gray old gabled house has been converted into a workshop, and a beautiful Gothic guildhall half turns its back upon a giant factory.

It was in this half-modern, half-ancient town of Ghent that Maurice Maeterlinck was born in 1862; and to those who are familiar with his writings it is evident that his early surroundings laid firm hold upon his thoughts. The son of Roman Catholic parents, he was sent for his education to the local Jesuit college, where, no doubt, it was hoped that his steps would be guided toward the priesthood. And, indeed, of the eighteen boys in his special class eleven followed this traditional course. But

THE MYSTICISM OF MAETERLINCK

Maeterlinck revolted. Although, like his transatlantic master and acknowledged guide, he

> Liked a church and liked a cowl,
> And loved a prophet of the soul;
> Yet not for all his faith could see
> Would he a cowléd churchman be.

To please his father he agreed to study law, although his thoughts were evidently far afield throughout the process. One case he argued and no more, and that he lost; after which he gave himself to the pursuit of letters. A vague, wild, fearful bit — *The Slaughter of the Innocents* — ushered him upon the field of literary strife, where now we are free to think how great a slaughter of innocent hope and promise it would have been, had parental influence sufficed to enclose and cramp him either in the church or the courthouse.

But when we have chronicled these outward facts of age, inheritance, and education, setting him down as a Belgian by birth, and a man of letters by brave resistance to familiar household foes, we are beset by difficulties. Further classification is not easy. Where does Maeterlinck belong among the authors of the world, and how shall we describe him? He has written plays and he has written poetry; he is the author of essays and of biographical sketches. His writings include things spiritual as well as things scientific. He has dealt, in the most convincing way, with spiritual beauty; but perhaps the best of all his books is a scientific study of the humble and familiar bee. It may be because of this wide variety in his writings that he has been claimed by many schools and classified under many heads. He is called a symbolist, a moralist, a mystic, a clever dramatist, a spiritual essayist, a poet writing in the medium of prose, a naturalist and man of science who carelessly assumes the clothes of a philosopher. He has been likened to Marcus Aurelius, Plotinus, Madame Guyon, Walt Whitman, Edgar Allan Poe, Emerson, and others; and the caustic Bernard Shaw has accused people of endeavoring to confer upon him the "Order of the Swan." Latterly he has been described as "the greatest living poet of love, if not the greatest poet of love that ever lived." And none of these appellations is without some reason to support it. In his love of the weird and gruesome he has some kinship with Poe. In his meditative vein he shows descent from the great Aurelius. I am not familiar enough with Walt Whitman to be able to pass upon his affinity there, but any one can recognize in his writings the influence of Tauler, Ruysbroeck, and their school.

One reason for these similarities is found, perhaps, in the fact, which may here be noted, that Maeterlinck is a persistent but discriminating

THE MYSTICISM OF MAETERLINCK

borrower. He knows a good thing when he sees it, and he is not above being helped and taught by others. What he receives, however, it is hardly necessary to add, he thoroughly transforms and makes his own. Taking the crude, unminted metal, he passes it through the furnace of his glowing fancy and stamps it with a glory that it did not have before. Thus in his play of *Mary Magdalene* he as frankly confesses himself indebted for two central features of the drama to Heyse's *Maria von Magdala*, and he as frankly tells us in the preface that, when he wrote to Heyse and asked permission to use and develop the situations, his request was curtly and even threateningly refused. *Monna Vanna*, it has been pointed out, "owes its *milieu*, and one of its structural features, to Browning's *Luria*, while *Pelléas and Mélisande* finds its roots in Dante's story of 'the two who go forever on the accursed air.'" Moreover, there can be no question of the kinship of *The Blue Bird* with *Peter Pan;* and the Belgian playwright, I believe, has bestowed on Mr. Barrie the title of godfather to the play. The greatest similarity, however, is undoubtedly with Emerson, who was himself so broad and free a borrower. Indeed, it is not without good reason that Maeterlinck has been hailed as the "European Emerson." Oftentimes, when you compare selected passages from the essays or writings of the two men, it is difficult to guess offhand which one of them is speaking. Which of them said this, for instance: "Man is always throwing his praise or blame on events, and does not see that he only is real, and the world his mirror and echo. He imputes the stroke to fortune, which in reality himself strikes"? Those of us who have explored the treasure-chambers of *The Buried Temple* would perhaps select this as one of the gems to be discovered there. As a matter of fact, it occurs in Emerson's *Sovereignty of Ethics*. Again we read: "There are certain fastnesses within our soul that lie buried so deep that love alone can venture down, and it returns laden with undreamed jewels whose lustre can only be seen as they pass from our open hand to the hand of one we love." That, we think, sounds familiar, and we search the essays on the *Over-Soul* and *Love;* but we must turn to the pages of *Wisdom and Destiny* to find it. Maeterlinck declares: "What I *say* often counts for little; but my presence, the attitude of my soul, my future and my past, that which takes birth in me and that which is dead. . . . All this it is that speaks to you at that tragic moment." And who, as he reads, can help thinking of Emerson's declaration: "What you *do* speaks so loud that I cannot hear what you say. Character speaks over our head. The infallible index of true character is found in the tone man takes." Again, there is Maeterlinck's description of the "inevitable self" that waits to meet us at the end of all our journeys: "Whether you climb up the mountain or go down the hill to the valley, whether you journey to the end of the world or merely walk around your house, none but yourself shall you meet on the highway of fate. If Judas goes forth to-night, it is towards Judas that his steps will tend." And Emerson, we know, agreed with him: "Travelling," he says, in speaking of self-reliance, "is a fool's paradise. I pack my trunk, embrace my friends, embark on the sea, and at last wake up in Naples, and there beside me is the stern fact, the sad self, unrelenting, identical, that I fled from. I seek the Vatican and the palaces. I affect to be intoxicated with sights and suggestions, but I am not intoxicated. My giant goes with me wherever I go." So there are other similarities which are too numerous to name. We remember Emerson's verses:

> Yon ridge of purple landscape,
> Yon sky between the walls,
> Hold all the hidden wonders
> In scanty intervals.

And we wonder if Maeterlinck did not have them somewhere in the back of his mind when he wrote: "There are eternal crevices even in the humble walls of a hovel, and the smallest windows cannot take away a line or a star from the immensity of heavenly space."

But enough! As these quotations indicate, there can be no doubt of how Maeterlinck would classify himself if he were granted that extraordinary privilege. He is a mystic, pure and simple. As a mystic he began to write, and as a mystic he reveals himself in all his more important works and studies. But before I go on to estimate him in this light, and to make a more careful analysis of his teaching, let me justify myself by his own deliberate words and judgment, and then let me hurriedly remind you of the essential teaching and the historical method of the mystics of all ages.

First of all let it be said that, whether he makes good the title or not, Maeterlinck considers himself a genuine mystic. He is confident of his inheritance, and claims descent from Ruysbroeck and Tauler, from Philo and Swedenborg and Fox — believing himself no foundling nor a son by mere adoption, but a spiritual heir. In his early writings he speaks enthusiastically of the great Plotinus, who, he declares, "of all the intellects known to me draws nearest to the divine." He quotes from Porphyry and the gnostics as if he had fed his soul upon their writings and had not simply dipped into their mystic shadows, as so many are content to do. Moreover, in his writings he has carefully justified and eloquently defended the mystic philosophy and teaching. "Many people," he says, "take it for a wild, dark

THE MYSTICISM OF MAETERLINCK

dream, crossed with vivid flashes of lightning, whereas, I believe that the writings of the mystics are the purest diamonds in the vast treasures of humanity; their truths have a strange privilege over ordinary truths, for they neither grow old nor die; and whether they come from India or Greece, they have neither country nor date, and wherever we meet them they are calm and real as God himself." "We are dealing here," he adds, "with the most *exact* of *sciences*, and not with a dream, for dreams have no roots, while the glowing flower of divine metaphysics has its mysterious roots in Persia and in India, in Greece as well as Egypt." These, it is clear enough, are the words of a man who believes that he has found the philosophy of life, containing definite truths of the deepest spiritual nature.

Of mysticism in general I need to speak in none but the briefest possible way, and that for the simple sake of clearness. We shall agree, I suppose, that mysticism is one of the many paths in life which lead to God. More than this, it is not merely one of the paths, it is the straightest path, and, according to those in every age who have found it out and gone that way, it leads directly into the presence of the Holy and Divine. The mystic is one who looks within, lives within, and loves to interpret all things from the standpoint of the soul. He believes in the supreme guidance of the "inner light," and holds to the necessity of trusting instinct, and honoring emotion. While the naturalist looks without, the mystic peers within; while the man of science studies the phenomena of outward nature, the mystic is absorbed with the phenomena of human nature. The one inquires, the other dreams; the first compares and classifies occurrences in the natural world, the second composes himself and contemplates things in the spiritual world which is centred in himself. Always, however, the true mystic pursues this inward path with one great end in view; and because of the gaining of that end he has secured the attention of the world. That end is the consciousness of the divine, and a conviction that God is the great Reality. "The mystics," says Professor Rufus Jones, in his recent and most rewarding volume entitled *Studies of Mystical Religion*, "in all ages and in all lands — *semper et ubique* — have been intent on finding a direct way to God"; and he adds, in the introduction to his book, "I shall use the word mystic to express the type of religion which puts the emphasis on immediate awareness of relations with God, on direct and intimate consciousness of the Divine Presence. It is religion in its most acute, intense, and living stage." "Moreover," he says, "it has been the contention of mystics in all ages that God Himself is the ground of the soul, and that in the deeps of their being all men partake of one central life. The genuine mystic, therefore, no more wants arguments to prove God's existence than the artist wants arguments to prove the reality of beauty, or the lover to prove the worth of love."

From all of this, and a great deal more that might be said or quoted, it appears that mysticism is a path of life, or avenue of thought, which, when properly pursued, conducts to a definite goal. It is a process, but it is likewise an end; it is a way of approach to truth along which, or more particularly at the end of which, one central and commanding truth has always been discovered. The way is the way of the individual soul, — along the shadowy road of quiet introspection, — but it ever has been held to lead to the consciousness of the Over-soul.

Accepting, then, as accurate these modern definitions of mysticism and its method, we go on to inquire in what sense Maeterlinck may properly be classed as a member of this historic and highly honored school. To what extent and how accurately may he be looked upon as a follower of Plotinus and Swedenborg and a true disciple of Emerson?

Now, that Maeterlinck believes in the path that has been trodden in all ages by the mystics of the world there cannot be the slightest doubt. In all his leanings toward the shadowland of Self, in all his love for things unseen, in all his praise of silence, too, and his perception of the treasures that the humble hold, our author is undoubtedly a mystic. He follows in the footsteps of those seers and solemn prophets of the soul who have declared, since the earliest time of human thought, that "within is the fountain of life" — that within is to be found the secret of contentment and the soul of truth. A Latin motto which is said to be written over his study door fitly gives expression to his faith. The motto may be translated:

> Whoever turns his outer sense
> To see his soul aright,
> He hears when no one speaks to him,
> Walks seeing through the night.

Yes, in the methods he pursues, as in the cravings of his nature, this Belgian thinker is distinctly mystical. Leave him alone for a moment, and he loses himself amid the heavy shadows that are cast by the pointed arches of some buried temple in the depths of human life; let his footsteps take their natural course, and they lead him along the winding pathways of that "double-garden," one-half of which extends across the sloping hillside of the human soul. *La vie intérieure* is his first and last and, it sometimes seems, his only real concern. The supreme aim of life, he tells us, is to "keep open the great road that leads from the seen to the unseen." As some one has written of him, he "comes with gentle words of wise and aspiring sincerity to impress upon the world the belief that the development and disclosure of the human soul is the ultimate aim and goal of existence." Here, in a nutshell, and phrased in his own enticing way, is his teaching in this regard. "I have grown to believe," he writes, "that an old man, seated in his armchair, waiting patiently with his lamp beside him, giving unconscious ear to all the eternal laws that reign about his house, interpreting without comprehending the silence of doors and windows and the quivering voice of the light, submitting with bent head to the presence of his soul and of his destiny — I have grown to believe that he, motionless as he is, does yet live in reality a deeper, more human, and more universal life, than the lover who strangles his mistress, the captain who conquers in battle, or the husband who avenges his honor."

Again, to give another illustration of his thought, it is natural that such a man, when writing of so universal yet so personal a thing as justice, should seek and find it in the secret place that is dearest and most familiar to him. "Justice," he says, "had been imagined everywhere except in man. It had dwelt in the sky. It had lurked behind rocks, it had governed the air and the sea, it had peopled an inaccessible universe. Then at last we peered into its imaginary retreats, we pressed close and examined; its throne of clouds tottered, it faded away; but at the very moment we believed it had ceased to be, behold, it reappeared and raised its head once more in the very depths of our heart."

Moreover, Maeterlinck is a mystic in this respect, that his books have hardly an impress of an epoch. Although a volume bears the title of *The Measures of Time*, his thoughts, his words, his innermost teachings, are practically timeless. It has been truly said of his books that most of them might have been "conceived and written a thousand years ago, and might equally, no doubt, be produced in any one of the thousands of years to come." So, too, he is a mystic in his occasional lapses into the exaggerated, the foolish, and grotesque — a respect in which the mystics have always sinned most gravely. Thus Angelus Silesius, a daring mystic of the seventeenth century, declared: "I know that God cannot live a moment without me. If I perish he must for want of me give up the ghost. I am as important to Him as He to me. I help maintain His being, as well as He mine." Emerson approached him when he declared, "The simplest person who in his integrity worships God becomes God," and added, "I become a transparent eyeball. I am nothing. I see all."

Maeterlinck's exaggerations run along a different

THE MYSTICISM OF MAETERLINCK

line, and he leans over the edge of sanity, particularly when he deals with death. "Our death," he says, "is the mould in which our life flows; it is death that has shaped our features. Of the dead alone should portraits be painted, for it is only they who are truly themselves." And again he says, "Whoever meets me knows all that I have done and shall do; — nay, he knows the very day on which I shall die." Of wisdom such as this we may well cry despairingly with the Psalmist, "Such knowledge is too wonderful for me; it is high, I cannot attain unto it."

But if Maeterlinck is a genuine mystic in such respects as these, and in others that we shall take account of later, let us pause here and make it evident that in the supremest sense of all — so far as arriving at the goal which the mystics of all ages have felt convinced that they reached — he distinctly and definitely fails. The old story tells us that the Magdalene went down to the dew-swept garden in the early morning light and found one waiting for her at the gate whom she took at first to be the gardener, but who turned out to be the very Saviour of her soul. And so it has been throughout the centuries, as we have seen, with the men and women whom we speak about as mystics. Their distinction has been always this, — that the way they went has brought them to the very presence of the Highest. With

Maeterlinck, however, although his "thoughts all gravitate in a visionary way to the Eternal, to the Absolute," he yet never finds, nor feels, himself face to face with a Supreme and Eternal Being who is both creator and inspirer of life. He goes down ever and again into the spacious garden of the soul, and he loves to walk and watch there. He caresses the shadows, and converses with the flowers. The bees are humming in the heavy afternoon of speculative thought, and he sees them store away the honey in the cells of quiet contemplation. But in all his musing, and his sense of mystery, he meets no shadowy form who asks for recognition, and to whom he cries out in an ecstasy of joy, "Rabboni."

Maeterlinck, in other words, is a mystic, but a mystic who does not arrive. He sets forth on the historic road, but fails to turn up at the historic goal. He takes the well-worn path on which other pilgrims have journeyed with joy because of what it led to; but with him not joy, but fear, is met along the way which leads him nowhere in particular. Never, for example, in the writings of this so-called mystic do you find an exultant cry like that of Emerson: "O my brothers, God exists! There is a soul at the centre of Nature and over the will of every man, so that none of us can wrong the universe. The whole course of things goes to teach us faith. We need only obey." Nowhere

THE MYSTICISM OF MAETERLINCK 157

does he proclaim the assurance that man can acquaint himself at first-hand with deity. Instead, what do we find? Only a heavy silence as to the mystery of mysteries,—the Power supreme above us all. When we come to the end of what he has to say, we see before us a question mark. Here, for example, is a case in point. In *The Buried Temple* he declares: "It was well that the Poet who found in his God an unquestionable ideal should incessantly hold before us this definitive ideal. But to-day, if we look away from the truth, from the ordinary experiences of life, on what shall our eager gaze rest?" Again, we come upon some cryptic utterance like this: "It is not the incomprehensible in Nature that masters and crushes us; but the thought that Nature may possibly be governed by a conscious, superior, reasoning Will — one that, although superhuman, has yet some kinship to the will of man."

Moreover, and what is worse, there are other connections in which he seems distinctly unreligious. Instead of finding God as the result of his quest, what he reveals is nothing but a subconscious, or a higher, self. "Within us," he says, "is a being that is our veritable ego; — our firstborn; immemorial, illimitable, universal, and probably immortal. Our intellect, which is merely a kind of phosphorescence that plays on this inner sea, has as yet faint knowledge."

Yes, it is self, mysterious, hooded, veiled, incomprehensible self that he finds at the end of all his inner searchings; and in this self his teachings find a centre. There is neither good nor evil, neither pain nor pleasure, neither ease nor hardship, neither calamity nor happiness, — except as thinking, and our inmost feelings, make them so.

Maeterlinck, I repeat, therefore, is less clearly a mystic than a mystic who does not arrive. He believes, so he tells us, in a faculty in man higher than intelligence, a faculty which he calls "mystic reason"; but that faculty, wonderful as it is, cannot penetrate the veil, or conduct us through the realm of shadows into light. Though it discloses wonders, it knows nothing about One who is the source of wonder; and though it recognizes beauty, it knows nothing of One who is the architect of beauty.

In the ancient temple of Edfu, the most symmetrical and best preserved of all the old Egyptian temples, one is led along through gateway after gateway, from outer sunlight, fierce and glaring, into shadow and then into deeper shadow, until one moves in almost utter darkness. Chamber opens into chamber, each one at a slightly higher level than the one preceding. Outside, behind the towering pylons, where the people gathered, is the spacious open court, roofed in by the azure sky. Within, at the opposite and furthermost extremity,

THE MYSTICISM OF MAETERLINCK

is the Holy of Holies, open to the priests alone, where the statue of the god was niched. It is a fascinating temple to explore, and at last, when the heavy gloom has silently embraced one, when chamber after chamber has been reached, and hall after hall been left behind, one comes to that holiest of holy chambers, with its solemn little niche — a niche of dark and solid granite in a dark and silent room. It is a dramatic moment, and one which comes to be the more dramatic when one discovers that the niche is — *empty!* The statue of the god is no longer there. His worship ceased long since, and the image was thrown down, broken, and destroyed.

Thus it is in the temple of thought that Maeterlinck has built. It is a perfect structure in its way, and enriched by the highest art. It is dim and suggestive, too, with shadowy corridors that open toward the sacred shrine of life. But the niche in the Holy of Holies is an empty niche; there is nothing there. If we worship, we must worship an abstraction; if we kneel, it must be before a reach of dark and impenetrable wall.

Moreover, the analogy of the Egyptian temple, with its passages that lead one into solemn darkness, suggests another truth which is characteristic of Maeterlinck. The ordinary mystic pursues his way along the hidden avenues of life, but comes out at the last upon a bright and broadening plain.

He plunges into secret darkness, but rejoices to have found thereby a glorious light. With our Belgian philosopher, however, the gloom is never lightened, the shadow never left behind. The darkness is what he revels in; and, with the darkness, all forms and fears and strange forebodings that cannot bear the light. Whether or not he is fond of shuddering himself and finds in it a species of religious awe, he is fond of making others shudder and grow cold. He is master of the art of stimulating the creepy feelings of life. In some of his plays he seems anxious to set forth mystery as something that is altogether terrifying. We see people huddled together at a window out of which they fear to look, or pressing against a door which they dread to open.[1] The scene is generally laid on the edge of a dark and pathless wood. In the play which he called *The Blind* the people are lost in a forest, and in *Pelléas and Mélisande* the lovers first encounter one another in a lonely and distant glade. The shadows are heavy. The dusk is everywhere. The sun is setting, — in fact, it has never fully risen. But if the gloom of the silent forest is on one side of his plays, the gloom of the stormy ocean, with tumbling waves that roll in from a boundless deep, is on the other. The ocean is always lashed into fury by a storm, while the sky is dark and full of thunder. Situ-

---

[1] A. Symons, *The Symbolic Movement in Literature*, page 158.

THE MYSTICISM OF MAETERLINCK

ated thus, between the two great natural symbols of impenetrable mystery, the poet pictures for us a dark and gloomy castle which is half in ruins. In the courtyard of the castle, or perhaps by the edge of the forest, there is a deep, black well, and beneath the crumbling castle walls we are led along dismal passageways and creaking corridors into silent crypts and gloomy dungeons. All the time the wind is howling, and the waves of the troubled sea are beating at the gates, and threatening to burst through the habitation man has built.

I remember that as a child I used to be strangely fascinated by the title of a book which stood upon the library shelves at home. I cannot recall that I ever opened it, and to this day I do not know exactly what it dealt with; but it was called *The Night Side of Nature*. That is the side of nature which appeals to Maeterlinck; and it is the side of human nature, too. His very characters are shadows, and when we strive to grasp their meaning they fade away into nothingness. Now all of this is mystical in the popular and superficial sense of being hazy and indistinct; but philosophically mystical it is not. The genuine mystic always deals with life — with soul-life and with life in heaven, if you will, but still with life. Maeterlinck, however, is forever exploring the spaces of the soul, where death and gloom, not life and light, are what prevail. Some one has called him a "meteorologist of the soul"; and so he is. But like many another of the ordinary craft it is storms and tempests that he usually reports.

It is interesting to notice, however, that within recent years he has left definitely behind him this morbid attitude of youth. In place of a dread of the unknown has come trust, and an almost superstitious awe has yielded to complacent confidence. In other words, he has gradually shaken off the shadow of the Jesuit college where he studied and has come out into the noonday of the twentieth century. So much is this the case that critics, who are always bound to find some fault, are now complaining of his easy optimism, and are tearing rents in what they think the flimsy garments of his latter-day philosophy. But the change has really been a growth, and a natural and wholesome one at that. What is more, it has made him in some respects a truer mystic than he was at first. He himself has given expression to this change, and says:

"It is consoling to observe that you follow the same route as the soul of this great world; that we have the same intentions, the same hopes, the same tests, and almost — except for our dreams of justice and pity, which is our own specific work — the same feelings. . . . That is why our attitude in the face of the mystery of these forces is

THE MYSTICISM OF MAETERLINCK

changed. It is no longer that of fear, but of courage. It is no longer the kneeling of a slave before his master, but it permits the look of equal to equal; for we carry within ourselves the equal of the most profound and the greatest mysteries."

And yet I do not say all this in the spirit of foolish criticism. I am not of those who are disposed to quarrel with talent, and least of all with genius; especially when the genius is one that seeks the mystery of the soul for inspiration, and proclaims the saving grace of individual character. Moreover, Maeterlinck being a mystic who does not arrive, he seems to me particularly typical of the age in which we live. Like all great writers, he voices the unspoken feelings of his time; and among the interesting phenomena of the particular period in which we live is the somewhat depressing fact that while the thirst for the divine remains unchanged, the means for the slaking of that thirst appear to be taken from us. People wish to believe, but often cannot. They have religion, or something which passes for it, but oftentimes are not religious. How many are the people who might fitly be described as agnostic mystics! They have the instincts and desires which fired and inspired saints and seers of old; but far too often they find themselves compelled to go without the glorious vision and the all-sustaining faith.

In this respect our Belgian prophet is among the

most modern of all writers, reflecting the doubts and wonderings of his day. But while perhaps the most significant thing about him as a mystic is the one that I have pointed out, it would be a mistake, and, worse than a mistake, it would be a grave injustice to ourselves and him to pass over without emphasis many other features in his teachings that are hardly less distinctive, and of very positive worth. Although he may not reach the mystic goal and achieve direct vision of the Highest, yet on the way he has seen and taught us things of great importance. His very "glorification," as Chesterton calls it, "of the inside of things at the expense of the outside," is not only a corollary of his mystical bent of mind, but a corollary which calls for every emphasis that can possibly be given. Welcome, indeed, in these days of superficial, and often silly, materialism, is the prophet of a scientific mysticism; and thrice welcome at a time when most of us are intent on improving the mere conditions of life is a well-accepted teacher who enforces the supremacy of life itself. The value of Maeterlinck's teaching, therefore, has the general value of all teaching that calls attention to self-reliance, self-development, and the need of spiritual culture. And it has much more than this. Under the spell of his genius the importance of the life within is given fresh interpretation and has taken on a dignity and glory which hardly had been given it before.

THE MYSTICISM OF MAETERLINCK

Most important, perhaps, but at any rate of genuine value and significance, is the teaching of this man in regard to the soul's relationship, or attitude, to trouble and disaster. He gives new emphasis and meaning to the old assertion that "the soul is its own refuge, and its own defence." Nowhere does he rise so close to ecstasy, or glow with such a fervor of conviction, as when he pictures a human soul facing some terrible and inevitable calamity and calmly defying it, saying in substance to the shadowy form, as it approaches, "You can have no power over me except as I supply the weapons." That is dramatic and sublime. For how often do people exaggerate and arm their troubles, making them terrible indeed, and capable of inflicting mortal wounds! "Physical suffering apart," he says in *Wisdom and Destiny*, "not a single sorrow exists that can touch us except through our thought; and whence do our thoughts derive the weapons wherewith they attack or defend us? We suffer very little from suffering itself; but from the manner wherein we accept it, overwhelming sorrow may spring."

Less unique, and much more commonplace, is his constant reiteration of the fact that the soul is the source and seat of all true content and happiness. This trite and familiar truth is lifted out of the dust of what is familiar and outworn, being presented to us at the hand of genius in new and shining garments. "All men can learn to be happy," he assures us, "and the teaching of it is easy. . . . Smiles are as catching as tears, and periods men have termed happy were periods when there were some who knew of their happiness. . . . There is more joy in the smallest joy whereof we are conscious than in the approach of the mightiest happiness that enters not into our soul."

Again, Maeterlinck stands for what we may call the democracy of the moral life. He believes in the Republic of the Soul. The world within, as he sees it, pays little attention to the ethical gradations and classifications which are so distinctive of our class-morality. "Not to all men," he reminds us, "is it given to be hero or genius, victorious, admirable always, or even to be simply happy in exterior things; but it lies in the power of the least-favored among us to be loyal, and gentle, and just; to be generous and brotherly; — he that has least gifts of all can learn to look on his fellows without envy or hatred, without malice or futile regret; the outcast can take his strange, silent part (which is not always that of least service) in the gladness of those who are near him; and he that has barely a talent can still learn to forgive an offence with an ever nobler forgiveness."

He applies the same deep principle to degrees of insight, or revelation, believing with Emerson,

> There is no great, and no small,
> To the Soul that maketh all.

"Not an evening passes," he is convinced, "but the smallest thing suffices to ennoble the soul"; and he is very sure, as he says in *The Treasure of the Humble*, "that the day you lingered to follow a ray of light through a crevice in the door of life, you did something as great as though you had bandaged the wounds of your enemy, for at that moment you no longer had any enemies."

Maeterlinck has stood very attentively and reverently close up to the narrow wall that separates the finite from the infinite, the human from the divine. If he has not heard certain voices that have always seemed of chief significance, let us at least be thankful that he has told us honestly what he does hear, and in language of transcendent beauty. The world is full enough of echoes, and it is hardly worth our while to pay attention to them. But when a living voice is raised that tells of personal revelation, and expresses some of our unuttered longings, we may wisely stop and pay attention. And in the meantime we may well believe that not yet has this thinker given us his full or final word. It is much to be hoped that it is with him, as with the fine patrician house in Bruges which bears, he has told us, on beams and pediment the suggestive device — "Within me there is more."

At least, it is certainly significant of this author that he has taken for his summer home the picturesque ruins of an ancient Abbey. When the monks were banished from France in 1907, Maeterlinck leased from the State the Abbey of St. Wandrille in Normandy, not far from Havre; and there in deserted monastic halls the lengthening shadows deepen around him.

BY WAY OF CONTRAST

BY WAY OF CONTRAST[1]

THE author of the Book of Ecclesiasticus advised that we should "praise famous men, and the fathers that begat us." "The Lord," he said, "had wrought great glory by them by his great power from the beginning." As Americans we have not been slow to act on the advice. What we are to-day as a people, with the standards we uphold, and the ideals we pursue, we are in large part because of our two most famous men. I refer, of course, to Washington and Lincoln.

It is interesting and important to remember that these men are the two great products of our new and freer civilization, who have long since commanded the attention of the entire world. Europeans have been somewhat inclined to affect, if they have not always had, an ignorance of American history and life! Speak of Adams, or of Jefferson, or of Alexander Hamilton to the average Frenchman or Italian, or even Englishman, and he gazes at you with entire blankness. But of Washington and Lincoln he is very far from ig-

[1] From *The Letters of William Roscoe Thayer* (page 321) it appears that this paper was read before the Thursday Evening Club of Boston, February 21, 1918. The manuscript, as left by the author, bears unmistakable signs of later revision.

norant. He compares them gladly to his own great men and leaders. Indeed, as often as the gaze of Europe has been directed toward the West, it has been lifted in astonishment to meet the mountainous attainments of these two great men, — and now much more so than ever in the past.

As it happens, these two great men of ours, whom the whole world has agreed to praise, were the contemporaries respectively of two great men in Europe, both of whom were Germans! Washington lived in the same age with Prussia's patron-hero, Frederick the Great, although twenty years his junior; and Lincoln, the great Emancipator, was only six years older than Bismarck, the builder of an empire.

It will, I think, be helpful and instructive to compare these men and to set in contrast the ideals for which they stood. We shall understand, I think, a little better the influences that led up to the World War, if we look at the differing natures of the men whom these countries have agreed to praise.

Washington and Frederick the Great, as I have said, were contemporaries. Their lives overlapped considerably in point of time: but as far as justice and honor and all that we know as character are concerned, they must remain as far apart as the poles.

When Washington was a young surveyor, stak-

BY WAY OF CONTRAST

ing out claims in the wilderness of the Allegheny Mountains, Frederick was surveying with satisfaction the territory that he had just treacherously stolen from the young Empress, Maria Theresa! When Washington was making his way through the woods with Braddock's expedition, and trying to warn that general against the cunning of the savages, Frederick was preparing to defend himself against a coalition of peoples who were determined to punish him for his savage and unscrupulous rapacity! By the time that Washington came to the front and took command of the forces that defied the tyranny of a German king who was seated on the throne of England, Frederick had fastened a tyrannical form of government upon Prussia, and had proclaimed war to be that country's national industry.

"As I take it," wrote Carlyle, "universal history — the history of what man has accomplished in this world — is, at bottom, the history of the *great* men who have worked here. *They* were the leaders of men, these great ones: the modellers, patterns, and, in a wide sense, creators, of what the general mass contrived to do, or to attain; all things, that we see standing accomplished in the world, are properly the outward material result, the practical realization and embodiment, of thoughts that dwelt in the great men sent into the world."

And that is true! But not precisely as the confident Carlyle intended, who censured weakness more vehemently almost than wickedness, and to whom power seemed all-important — whether power for evil or for good!

If the United States and Germany found themselves far apart in 1914, it was because the fathers of the countries were so far apart in ideals and attainments. As Americans look back to Washington with reverence and pride, so Germany looks back to Frederick! And what both of us are, as Carlyle affirmed, is largely due to what these great ones — the leaders, the modellers, the creators of our separate countries — did and were.

Now, I take it we shall all agree in regard to the most fundamental characteristic in the performance, personality, and life of Washington. It has been said of him that "a grateful tradition has so recklessly transformed the character of Washington that he has become a kind of mechanical monster stuffed with incredible copy-book headings, strangely unlike the altogether human and passionate hero that he was in fact." But in spite of what adulation has done to disguise the man, it is not difficult to recognize his "integrity"! He could be trusted! When he gave his word, the word was kept! What he professed, he did! Men knew where to find him; and there are few great characters in history in whom there was

BY WAY OF CONTRAST

so little guile. "I do not remember," he said of himself in 1786, "that in the course of my life I ever forfeited my word, or broke a promise made to any one."

Moreover, the principle that he believed in, and was proud to think that he had acted on in private life, was the principle that he recommended to the nation, and counselled the country to pursue! In his farewell address to the people of America, Washington used these memorable words: "Observe good faith and justice towards all nations; cultivate peace and harmony with all. Religion and morality enjoin this conduct; and can it be that good policy does not equally enjoin it? It will be worthy of a free, enlightened, and, at no distant period, a great nation, to give to mankind the magnanimous and too novel example of a people always guided by an exalted justice and benevolence! ... So far as we have already formed engagements, let them be fulfilled with perfect good faith! I hold the maxim no less applicable to public than to private affairs, that 'honesty is always the best policy.'"

From these counsels of political perfection, given by the Father of his Country, let us turn to the conduct and the counsels presented by the Father of that other Country, whose descendants have looked to him as proudly and as reverently as we have looked to Washington.

Said the Kaiser, "From childhood I have been influenced by five men — Alexander the Great, Julius Cæsar, Theodoric II, Frederick the Great, and Napoleon. Each dreamed of world empire. They failed. I have dreamed of German world-dominion and my mailed fist shall succeed."

Carlyle, the Hero-Worshipper, before proceeding to burn incense to his idol, was forced to confess: "Frederic is by no means one of the perfect demi-gods; and there are many things to be said against him with good ground. To the last a questionable hero, with much in him one could have wished not there, and much wanting one could have wished."

I was interested the other day to turn back to Macaulay's famous essay written in 1842, on this man, whom Carlyle even could confess no demi-god! I had not read it for nearly thirty years. And, as I read, it seemed that I was reading a description of what took place in August, 1914, and not in the autumn of 1741. "The King of Prussia," says Macaulay, "the Arch-Macchiavel, had already fully determined to commit the great crime of violating his plighted faith, of robbing the ally whom he was bound to defend, and of plunging all Europe into a long, bloody, and desolating war! . . . He determined to assemble a great army with speed and secrecy, to invade Silesia before Maria Theresa should be apprised of his design, and to add that rich province to his king-

BY WAY OF CONTRAST

dom! . . . Without any declaration of war, without any demand for reparation, in the very act of pouring forth compliments and assurances of good-will, Frederick commenced hostilities! Many thousands of his troops were actually in Silesia before the Queen of Hungary knew that he had set up any claim to any part of her territories. The whole world sprang to arms! On the head of Frederick is all the blood that was shed in a war which raged during many years, and in every quarter of the globe! . . . The evils produced by his wickedness were felt in lands where the name of Prussia was unknown; and, in order that he might rob a neighbor whom he had promised to defend, black men fought on the Coromandel, and red men scalped each other by the Great Lakes of North America."

As we listen to those words, we cannot but think how history repeats itself! Substitute "Belgium" for Silesia, and "William" for Frederick, and we have the story of 1914, — with its secrecy, its treachery, its sudden "spring at the throat of Europe," and its disregard for solemn promises! Truly, it is well to be careful whom we select as heroes; and to doubt whether to be "great" alone is sufficient to call forth our praises.

But history is not always written with impartial pen! It may be that this man, whom Prussia ever since has idolized, has been misjudged by perfidious and prejudiced historians. It might be possible to think so were it not that out of his own mouth he is both to be judged and then condemned.

Frederick did what Job so devoutly wished that his adversary had done, — he wrote a book! Here are some of the counsels that he set down for the future guidance of his country and her coming kings. Remember what Washington had advised his countrymen in regard to good faith and justice and the keeping of all national engagements, and then consider the significance of maxims such as these: "If there is anything to be gained by it we will be honest; if deception is necessary let us be cheats"; "Know once for all that in the matter of kingcraft, we take what we *can;* and that we are never wrong unless we have to give back what we have taken."

There is no exaggeration in all this. These sayings are recorded and set down in the *Memoirs* of the Mighty Frederick, where they were faithfully studied by the German people for a hundred years.[1]

Here is another specimen: "Since, then, it has been agreed upon among men that cheating one's fellow-men is a cowardly act, an expression has been sought for which might soften this act, and the word *politics* has been chosen. My dear

[1] See James Brown Scott, *A Survey of International Relations between the United States and Germany* (based on official documents).

BY WAY OF CONTRAST

nephew, by the word 'politics' I understand that we must seek to deceive others; it is a means of having the advantage; or, at least, of being on a par with the rest of mankind.

"This principle having been stated, never blush for making alliances with a view to your being the only one to draw advantage from them. Do not commit the stupid mistake of not abandoning them whenever you believe your interests are at stake: and especially maintain vigorously this maxim, — that to despoil your neighbors is to take away from them the means of doing you an injury.

"If we are desirous of entering into a treaty with other powers, and we remember that we are Christians, — we are undone!

"I venture to affirm that there are treaties which necessity, wisdom, prudence, or the welfare of the people, compel sovereigns to break.

"When our interests change, we must change our actions accordingly.

"When Prussia shall have made her fortune, she will then be able to assume an air of good faith and of constancy, such as, at the most, becomes only great states and little sovereigns. Unreservedly the King of Prussia must make war his principal industry."

What wonder that with maxims such as these to guide him, the nephew of this great man, and his successor on the throne, should have uttered, more than sixty years ago, an expression which recently has become famous. "All written constitutions," said the King of Prussia in 1847, "are but scraps of paper."

We might draw many other contrasts, should we care to do so, between the standards of actions and ideals of these two great men — the one the idol ever since of our proud Republic, the other the great example of political autocracy.

We remember, most of us, the hesitation and diffidence with which Washington accepted the position of Commander-in-Chief of the American forces. "I beg it may be remembered," he said, "that I declare with the utmost sincerity, I do not think myself equal to the command I am favored with."

Frederick, however, was frank enough to confess that his leading motives in provoking an unjust war were the love of fame and the desire to make a name for himself.

Washington was a deeply religious man, and counseled his countrymen not to think that morals without religion were secure, or that popular government could succeed without them both.

Frederick, however, could declare that "a king is unwise in having any religion. He must have maintained a respectable outward appearance in order to conform himself to those who surround him and take notice."

BY WAY OF CONTRAST

Wide apart in so many respects as the two men are, — a mighty gulf fixed between, — it is none the less a fact that they belong together in their absolute devotion to their respective countries. Washington, in bidding farewell to public office, and declining a third term in the Presidency, could refer to the "forty-five years that he had dedicated to the service of the country"; and, with equal truth, Frederick could call attention to his passionate devotion. He was ready to live or die, so only Prussia were made great! "He was a real shepherd of his people." He could say: "I have always regarded the revenues of the state as the ark of the covenant which no unholy hand ought to touch. I have never applied the public revenue to any private advantage."

Sharp, however, as was the conflict in ideals, in most respects, between the great American and the mighty Prussian of the eighteenth century, it was not more marked than the later contrast which the nineteenth century presented.

Abraham Lincoln and Otto von Bismarck were more nearly of age than Washington and Frederick; but in other respects they were no less far apart! The greatness of both men cannot be denied; but neither can the difference in their greatness! They belonged to the same generation, had the same amount of history to profit by, read the same Bible, prayed, ostensibly, to the same

God, — but with what different results! Both men towered in attainments far above contemporaries; but they were more widely separated in thought and actions from each other than they were from the lesser men whose leaders they became.

Bismarck was one of the great throne-builders of the ages! Lincoln, being dead, was placed before the throne of God; and "he that sitteth on the throne has spread his tabernacle over him."

Both men had to do with war; but how differently they approached it! In 1861, Lincoln pleaded with the Southern people who threatened to use force, as one might plead with children. "We are not enemies," he said, "but friends. We must not be enemies. Though passion may have strained, it must not break, our bonds of affection."

It was the boast of Bismarck, however, that he had personally forced three wars, and in each had been successful, by deceitful practices, in having his country seem to be the one attacked.

Each spoke the words by which he has come to be remembered. When we listen to Lincoln, we hear him saying, "With malice toward none; with charity for all." When Bismarck speaks, we hear the harsh words, "By blood and iron."

Lincoln once said to his friend Joshua Speed: "Speed, when I am gone, I want it to be said of me that I always plucked up a thistle and planted a flower — where I thought the flower would grow." Bismarck, in looking back from his height of power could confess: "I have made many people unhappy! But for me, three big wars would not have been fought, and 80,000 men would not have been slain. . . . From all that I have done, I have derived little or no joy."

It has been truly said of Lincoln that through all the fierce passions of civil strife, when hatred was so generally stirred, he never used a single phrase, or uttered one word of malice or of rancour, which might return to embitter the defeated combatants, or be resented by their descendants. It is true, that it was a civil, not a foreign war, that he lived through, and suffered so acutely in conducting. None the less, those who know Lincoln cannot doubt that under different circumstances it would have been the same. At least, we cannot picture any provocation which would have tempted him to say, with Bismarck, "Leave your enemies nothing but their eyes to weep with."

It is perhaps unnecessary to enlarge upon Lincoln's utter and unfailing honesty. A recent volume that has been written in his praise, is entitled *Honest Abe*. It is filled with a multitude of anecdotes setting forth Lincoln's inherent straightforwardness as neighbor, lawyer, and statesman. In contrast, we have but to mention the history of the well-known Ems despatch, which precipitated, if it did not cause, the Franco-Prussian War. It is hardly necessary to repeat the famous story. It is familiar to most people. Mention of it is to be found in the Lives of Bismarck, and his own memoirs, as well as elsewhere. It is true that the great statesman could declare that he neither changed nor added a single word to the original message from his king; but he so condensed it that his friends confessed that it had a wholly different ring. "Before," they said, "it sounded like a parley; now it is like a flourish in reply to a challenge." And Bismarck had so little conscience in regard to the act of falsification, that he narrated in his *Memoirs* all the circumstances under which the act was done, and what good appetites he and his friends had when the change was successfully wrought.[1]

But the real matter of importance, after all, and perhaps the more rightly to be considered in such days as these, is the essential and far-reaching difference between these two great men in political philosophy and principles of government.

Lincoln was, before all else, the Great Emancipator! He lifted up a race. He gave freedom to a people. He was essentially a Democrat. "Beyond his own country" his name is recalled as

---

[1] Sir Charles Dilke wrote: "Bismarck told me when I was staying with him in September, '89, that he deliberately altered the telegram by cutting it down 'from a telegram of 200 words which meant peace to a telegram of 20 words which meant war,' and in this form it was placarded through North Germany in every village." — *Life of Sir Charles Dilke*, I, page 157.

"the greatest among those associated with the cause of popular government." A plain man of the people himself, he believed in the people — in their honesty, intelligence, and capacity to rule themselves, and manage wisely their affairs! What is more, he believed in *all* the people, making no distinctions, whether in regard to sex, or color, or condition! Once, in his early days, during a political campaign, a newspaper demanded that all the candidates should show their hands. "Agreed," wrote Lincoln. "Here is mine!" And there followed a young man's avowal of advanced opinions: He would give the franchise to all who pay taxes, "not excluding females"! His whole doctrine as to government was expressed in a sentence which he wrote not long before he was elected President. It reads: "As I would not be a slave, so I would not be a master! This expresses my idea of Democracy. Whatever differs from this, to the extent of the difference, is no Democracy." And it remained for him, upon the field of Gettysburg, to sum up the entire matter, and to express for all future time the principles of popular government. He declared, in immortal phrase: "It is for us to be here dedicated to the great task remaining before us . . . that this nation, under God, shall have a new birth of freedom; and that government of the people, by the people, for the people, shall not perish from the earth."

By way of contrast we recall that it was the mission of Lincoln's great contemporary across the sea to work for a lifetime in the very opposite direction. With a persistency as great, a devotion as entire, and a success that was no less marked, he opposed the people's will. Bismarck's political creed was very brief. It consisted of two articles, — and no more. They were: "I believe in the supremacy of Prussia, and in absolute monarchy." "More royalist," says a writer, "than the King, he opposed every concession that might diminish by a hair's breadth the royal prerogative! Constitutional government, popular representation, whatever Liberals had been struggling and dying for since 1789, he detested. . . . Democracy he scoffed at! . . . When half the world was repeating the words Liberalism, Constitution, Equality, he insisted that firm nations must be based on facts, not phrases." [1] He openly condemned the right of public meeting as "furnishing democracy with bellows"; a free press he stigmatized as a "blood-poisoner." Paper constitutions were his abhorrence, and puppet kings an occasion for his mirth. If the Emperor of Germany could say with conviction and immunity in 1900: "There is only one law, and that is my will; whoever opposes me, I will crush," it was the great contemporary of Lincoln who supplied him with the power.

[1] Wm. R. Thayer, *Throne Makers*, pages 12, 14.

BY WAY OF CONTRAST

Bismarck's most memorable and most characteristic utterance is worth remembering entire. It was made in 1862, one year before the Gettysburg address. He said in the military committee of the Prussian House of Deputies: "Not by speeches, and resolutions of majorities, are the great questions of the time decided, — that was the mistake of 1848 and 1849, — but by blood and iron." He openly despised representative government with "its interminable clatter, its indiscreet meddling, and its whimsical revulsions of opinion," and he frankly placed his faith in the iron hand and rigorous suppression.

When the war came to an end, with Germany in defeat, it was supposed that autocracy had received its death-blow. When the Kaiser went into exile, and his people adopted a Republican form of government, it was assumed that Democracy was finally established everywhere in the saddle.

As we write, however, Mussolini is repeating Bismarck's scorn of representative government, and Italy finds herself with neither a free press nor a free people. Stranger than all else is the calm suggestion, freely made, that France will never recover stability until she, too, discovers a tyrant and submits to some new Napoleon.

EDWARD EVERETT HALE

EDWARD EVERETT HALE[1]

NO one who ever saw Edward Everett Hale could possibly forget him. No one who knew him could fail to be impressed by his powerful personality. Moreover, no one whom he had helped, or influenced, — and there were hundreds and thousands of such people, — could ever think of him except with gratitude and even reverence.

Physically, he was a big man! He was built on generous lines. Feet and hands were enormous. His head was Homeric. Much the same might be said of him mentally. He was large in his grasp of things — the very opposite of narrow, or limited in outlook. He cherished few prejudices. He kept himself free from sects and parties of all kinds. He was exalted enough to look beyond them. He enjoyed a wide horizon.

Nor was it different when it came to moral attainments and to spiritual influence. He had a host of followers, an army of admirers, and countless friends. His friend and contemporary, Thomas Wentworth Higginson, wrote of him: "Probably no man in America except Beecher aroused and

[1] From the Proceedings of the Massachusetts Historical Society for April, 1922.

stimulated so many minds as Hale, and his personal popularity was unbounded."

He was the youngest member of the class of 1839 at Harvard, entering college at the early age of 13! He outlived all his classmates, — most of them by many years, — and just as certainly he towered above them all in fame and influence. In all respects, therefore, Dr. Hale, as he came familiarly to be called, was a marked and famous man. And he was famous, among other things, for the multiplicity of his interests, and for the variety of departments in which he attained distinction. He was a minister of religion, a man of letters, and a social reformer, — and in each of these three lines he established a national and even an international reputation. Moreover, as a man of letters, he was a writer of popular fiction, an essayist, and a poet, as well as an historian.

In the line of Social Reform he was organizing a church club one day, setting on foot a society for helping immigrants the next day, and then on the third proving himself a Prophet among peace advocates by suggesting that a Permanent High Court should be established among the nations, and telling how it could be organized. And when it comes to his career as a Minister of Religion nothing is more distinctive of him than the way his influence ignored denominational barriers! Many of the readers of his books had no idea that the popular author of *The Man without a Country* was the popular pastor of a busy city church; and among those who did know, there were many who never dreamed that he belonged to the heretical sect of Unitarians.

No one, therefore, can consider the career of Dr. Hale, whether adequately or only briefly, without taking account of him in these separate lines. From early years to extreme old age, he was active in all three of them at once. He was all the time, — and almost equally, — man of letters, man of good works, and man of God! In this fact lay his strength as well as weakness — the secret of his success as well as the cause of such minor failures as he made in life. And yet, it is probably a mistake to say that he would have accomplished more by attempting less — that he would have harvested a better crop, if he had scattered seed with more careful hand! It is nearer the truth to say, that he achieved much because he was so inherently versatile, unceasingly active, and instinctively disposed to acts of helpfulness and service. It was as natural for him to want to help a fellow creature, as it was for him to write a story, or to preach a sermon. He did all three with spontaneous ease, and he did them all three at the same time throughout his long and active life.

Perhaps the most controlling and far-reaching

influence in the career of Dr. Hale is to be found in the fact that his father was the editor of a newspaper. It was one of the best newspapers of the day; but still, it was a newspaper! It required haste in preparation, and called for variety of printed matter, rather than careful statement or precision of detail. He said once of himself, that he was "cradled in the sheets of the *Boston Daily Advertiser.*" And the peculiar odor of the daily press could be detected in his doings to the end.

For instance, he was only about ten or twelve years old when his father brought him one day a brief publication in French, told him to make a translation, and promised to have it printed in the newspaper. The boy was nonplussed. He knew no French. But his elder sister knew a little. In accordance with the mother's advice, therefore, the two children betook themselves to a dictionary and worked out a translation, which was printed, in due season, in the newspaper. Thus he took his first step in the realm of Letters; and never afterwards did the art of publishing have any fear for him. He was always ready, at almost any moment, to write upon a great variety of subjects, and to translate impulse into action.

In college, he took his place quite naturally in the Literary Set; won two Bowdoin prizes; was in the first eight of the Phi Beta Kappa, and graduated second in his class, having been appointed Class Poet. Like most college youths, he read widely; and, unlike many, he read deeply! It was indicative of his intention, already taken, to become a minister, that we find him reading Emerson's *Nature*. "It's an odd sort of book," he set down in his diary, "but I like it better than most everyone else seems to; though to be sure there's a good deal in it that I can't understand."

Later on, in his senior year, he heard Emerson's famous Divinity School Address. His disapproval was even more distinctly expressed. "I did not like it at all," he wrote. "The sermon seemed to me in singularly bad taste. Mr. Emerson's stock of startling phrases concerning God, mind, soul, etc., is getting exhausted, and I think his reputation will fall accordingly." In all of this, we can see the influence of early training. He was reared in a very conservative school, and his parents found many to agree with them in thinking that the Concord Sage, with his Transcendentalism, was not wholly of a sound and balanced mind!

But in his junior year the college diary set down something much more significant than these literary criticisms — something which reveals the youth to have been, in a very characteristic and noble sense, the father of the man! Under September 14, 1838, occurs this entry: "I went to the poorhouse to see our old Goody, who has had a stroke of palsy." He went to the poorhouse, this lad of only sixteen, on an errand of helpfulness and mercy! I wonder how many of the other fellows, rooming in that college building, went to see in her weakness the paralyzed old woman who had made their beds and swept their rooms? Perhaps they *all* went, I don't know. But, what I *do* know is that for more than seventy years after that little act of courtesy and consideration, Edward Everett Hale of the Harvard Class of '39 was constantly, in one way or another, going to poorhouses, and to all sorts of out-of-the-way places — going everywhere, in short, where people needed help and could be given cheer! Then, and always afterwards, his was a life of eagerness to "Lend a Hand!" Indeed, so much was this the case that, more than eighty years later, Lyman Abbott could write of him as "an *American Abou Ben Adhem*," whose name "led all the rest," because of love for his fellow man!

There can be no doubt, therefore, as regards the fundamental and controlling impulse of his life! Whatever else he might be, and in later years was known to be, — whether author, story writer, historian, Prophet, or Reformer, — he was first and foremost a *minister!* He was an author because he was a Minister of Religion first, and except for the love of his fellow man he never would have been the Preacher, Prophet and Reformer, whose name and influence reached across the sea.

A son, who later came to be his biographer, has ventured to suggest that this American Abou Ben Adhem went into the Ministry of Religion because of the time he thus would have for literary work. He quotes certain sayings to sustain this view. But the point was not well taken. From early years it seems to have been assumed in the family that the boy was to enter the ministry and no decided "Step" was necessary, or implied, when he did so! From first to last he was a vitally religious man! His faith was not concerned with formulas, dogmas, or "Articles"; it was first-hand, personal, direct. As a young man he felt himself "called" to the work; and like many another Prophet he could look back to moments of definite inspiration. Just as Channing, when a youth in college, saw the heavens open in a Cambridge meadow underneath a clump of willows, and received what he called a "message from the Spirit," so it was with Edward Everett Hale. The account that he gave of the experience is well worth quoting. It deserves a place in mystical literature, and proves this Boston boy, just out of Harvard College, the spiritual heir of Francis of Assisi, of Fénelon, and of Madame Guyon. The experience occurred in 1844, and that he wrote it out more than half a century later, shows how deep an impression it had made — shaping, indeed, a whole long life.

"I was at Albany," he says, "where I had been very much alone. . . . Perhaps it was to this loneliness that I owe a revelation which stands out in my memories of life. I had been reading in my musty dark bed-room by an air-tight stove. I think I was reading the *Revue des Deux Mondes*. But I put the book down for what people used to call *Reflection*, and I saw, or perceived, or felt, that I was not alone, and could not be alone. This Present Power knows me, and loves me! I know Him, and love Him. He is here: I am here: we are together! And it is a companionship much closer than I could have with any human being sitting in that chair! Of course," he adds, "I do not mean that before this I had never prayed to God, or waited for an answer. But it is true that the sense of perfect, or absolute companionship — the give and take sense of society, took form in my life then, by the side of that rusty stove, and in that musty little room at the hotel Delavan, such as it had never taken before."

Thus this great man "experienced Religion" in his early manhood. It was an experience that never left him. He could no more forget the incident than Isaiah could forget his vision of "the throne that was high and lifted up," or Ezekiel the scene that took place by the river of Chebar; or the Apostle Paul the light that burst upon him as he journeyed to Damascus.

EDWARD EVERETT HALE

That mystical experience formed forever afterwards the central feature of his faith. His listeners heard him more than once affirm in his later years that he could put his whole creed into four words! Those words, he used to say with explosive emphasis, are these: "Our Father who art." Not *my* Father he used to go on and explain; not *your* Father; but "*our* Father." And not our Father who *wast*, in some distant past, long centuries ago; but "who *art*" — a living, constant Presence with us all!

In this simple faith, and guided by this thought, he carried on an active and effective ministry! Thirty years after the vision at the Delavan, when some one wrote and asked about his beliefs, and how faith could be secured, he answered: "For faith, the soul needs to pray simply to God, 'Father, help me'; that is quite enough!" But, he added, "you can no more argue a man into faith with the best of arguments than you can whip him into faith with the best of whips." Here is something that must be felt; that comes as a result of quiet thought and lonely meditation.

Moreover, it is not generally known that this mystic tendency to meditation was always strong in this restlessly active man. One of the great books on Mysticism is Vaughan's *Hours with the Mystics*. It is written in the form of dialogues, or conversations. A group of friends relate their experiences, and discuss historic visions. So Dr. Hale once undertook to carry on a correspondence with a highly gifted brother minister, in which each should reveal to the other his inmost musings, revelations, and spiritual feelings! It is a thousand pities that the press of life soon caused the correspondence to be discontinued. If it had been carried on at length, and published, it would have given evidence of a deeply spiritual, meditative, mystical side to one of the most energetic, busy men who ever lived!

With such a vivid consciousness of spiritual things, his ministry was bound to be a fruitful one. He served only two churches, — the Church of the Unity in Worcester for a period of ten full years; and then the South Congregational Society in Boston from 1856 until his death, — a period of more than fifty years. But all this time he served the whole community as well! He was an active minister-at-large, whose parish was the world — his "people" all whom he could help.

He used to set it down in his diary about once every year, that he was determined to curtail these outside interests, and confine himself to parish claims. But it could no more be than Amos could remain a herdsman in Tekoa, or than the great Apostle could resist the call from Macedonia! And yet, with endless outside interests, it is amazing how faithful he continued to parish needs, and denominational affairs. No man was ever less of a sectarian. Not a drop of bigot's blood was in his veins. He was always catholic in spirit; but he valued higher than anything else his Congregational inheritance. He was a confirmed Liberal and a conscientious Unitarian; but he claimed fellowship with Christians everywhere, and with human beings of all races!

When Booker Washington first came to Boston, — long before he had become famous, — a big man gave him a lift with his heavy travelling bag as he alighted from the train. A bewildered stranger in an unfamiliar northern city, the black youth, who was born in slavery, was then guided to a street car. The good Samaritan was Dr. Hale — always the friend of any one in need of help.

But in spite of his incessant service in the ministry, the name of Edward Everett Hale was getting all the time to be more and more the name of a man of letters. It would be difficult, if not quite impossible, to say just when he first came forward as an author. As we have seen, he was cradled in a newspaper, and the rattle most familiar to his early years was the rattle of the printing press. He was born among books, and pen and paper were his toys. It can be definitely said, however, that his first real success as an author came through his *Man without a Country*. And, as not infrequently happens, the book which first attracted attention, and securely made his reputation, still remains the most popular and famous that he ever wrote.

It was Dr. Hale's own opinion that the best of all his stories was *In His Name*. And that tale of the early Waldenses has the supreme advantage over nearly all his other works of fiction, in not being an *extravaganza*. It is neither whimsical nor farcical, — but simple, natural, and touching. I read it for the first time very recently, and it was with difficulty that I could bring myself to put it down until it had been finished.

Dr. Hale's general method in fiction can hardly be commended as the highest. It was his custom "to make a practically impossible assumption," — to outline, or picture, a situation that was outside the range of the credible, — "and then procced to tell the story in a logical and realistic manner." I imagine that his method grew out of the fact that he generally read these stories to church gatherings, or at Sunday-school entertainments. The first necessity on such rather dreary occasions is to catch the attention, and wake up the assembly. And this he did, somewhat to the detriment of literary art. But he did it with consummate skill, and it is an evidence of his genius that his *Man without a Country* was generally accepted as historic. From the day of its first appearance to the present moment, it has had a host of readers, and it taught a lesson that the growth of internationalism has not yet made unnecessary. Moreover, as a work of fiction it goes far to establish the soundness of the author's own estimate of where his true talent really lay. He often used to say of himself that he was by nature a story-teller.[1]

Perhaps it was because of this that he treated History as lightly as he did — caring more for the general sweep of events than for accuracy in detail. He loved nothing better in his later years than drawing on his memories, as he sought to make the past a living, throbbing, actual thing. But with the multitude of his interests, he could not, or did not, take the time to verify his statements, so that his stories, rather than his histories, redound to his literary reputation. He believed in original sources, but he was often in too much of a hurry to seek for them. In general, too, his dictum that history must first of all be interesting, caused him to lay too little emphasis on accuracy; while his memory, although remarkable, was not entirely infallible.

[1] It was in the story called *Ten Times One is Ten* that Dr. Hale first phrased the motto by which he came to be so widely known:

"To look up and not down,
To look forward and not back,
To look out and not in, and
To lend a hand."

The motto may be contrasted with a favorite aphorism of St. Bernard: *Respice, Aspice, Prospice,* — "Look back, look around, look forward."

But to many people Dr. Hale was neither minister nor man of letters, but first, and foremost, and forever, an indefatigable philanthropist, and leader in all phases of good work! There was hardly a movement for helping the poor, lifting up the fallen, recovering the lost, visiting the imprisoned and the fatherless, and generally for bringing light into socially dark places, that he did not champion and abet! For nearly fourscore years he was absolutely restless in his passion to be of use, to help along God's kingdom, to be about the "Father's business," and to "lend a hand." No one occupying a pulpit was ever more convinced than he that the Christian minister's first function was to engage in Christian work. The preaching of good sermons was of less importance in his eyes than the promotion of good causes.

And yet, with all his enthusiasm for human welfare he elaborated no scheme for social salvation. He promulgated no system of which he came to be the champion. He originated no new method of reform, like Arnold Toynbee, nor any pioneering work, like General Booth. Radical reforms, unpopular causes, failed to strike the spark of fire in his breast. He was brought up in a conservative social school. His mother, who was a sister of Edward Everett, could describe the spare room in the Hale household as "a Sanctum where the voice of the young pleader for the slave was never heard." This man, therefore, was not a theoretical, but a practical Reformer. He was a day-by-day worker for the right: not a slashing, critical exponent of the evils of the social system in the midst of which we live.[1] He set himself to cure troubles that were *near at hand*, and did not undertake to tell the world how all social troubles could be eliminated. In the matter of social diseases he was a "general practitioner," and not a surgical "specialist." He was the friend of *all* good movements, the fanatical exponent of no one in particular! As his old friend, Dr. Lyman Abbott, has written of him: "He was not a partisan of any party in either church or state; nor the enlisted adherent of any *cause*. He was not an Abolitionist, nor a Prohibitionist, nor a Socialist — nor was he enrolled in the ranks of their opponents. He was an advocate of many causes; but he did not belong to any organized body of Reformers."

[1] The following entry in the journal of his uncle, Edward Everett, is interesting:

Sunday, Feb. 27, 1859: To church all day. Young Mr. Hale preached with seriousness, earnestness, and a devotional spirit.

The poor young man is sadly behind the times. In the Music Hall, on the contrary, in the *Reverend* Theodore Parker's pulpit, Mr. Ralph Waldo Emerson read a lecture on "Natural Aristocracy." That may be called religious instruction. That is what poor, suffering, bereaved, heart-broken men and women want; that is the kind of teaching desirable for young men hurrying into life to purify their characters and enable them to govern their passions; that is what old men and women want who are just dropping into the grave, — the "natural Aristocracy"!

In all of this, however, there was one conspicuous exception; and because of this exception, he proved himself "A Prophet of the Twentieth Century"; and about as clear-eyed and farseeing a Prophet as recent centuries have seen. The name of Dr. Hale will probably be remembered longest in connection with World Peace, and because he foresaw a particular need if Peace were ever to be permanent. This need was that of a permanent *International Tribunal, — a Supreme Court of the Nations!* As early as 1885 he began to preach and prophesy upon the matter; and he never ceased his prophecies until death took him to the Judgment Seat of God. In 1889, in the course of a sermon entitled "The Twentieth Century," which was preached at Washington probably with some of the Supreme Court Judges before him in the congregation, he went for the first time with some detail into the subject. He said: "The Twentieth Century will apply the word of the Prince of Peace to international life. The wisdom of statesmen will devise the solution which soldiers and statesmen will accept with thankfulness. . . . The suggestion will come from one of the six great Powers. It will come from a nation which has no large permanent military establishment; that is, it will probably come from the United States. This nation, in the most friendly way, will propose to the other Great Powers to have, each one, a jurist of world-wide fame, who, with the other five, shall form a permanent tribunal of the highest dignity. Everything will be done to give this tribunal the honor and respect of the world. As an international court it will be organized without reference to any special case under discussion. Then it will exist! Timidly, at first, and with a certain curiosity, two nations will refer to it some international question — not of large importance — which has perplexed their negotiations. The tribunal will hear counsel, and will decide. Their decision will be the first in a series which will mark the great victory of the Twentieth Century."

Such was his prophecy when it first was made! He repeated it often. He elaborated it. He got people familiar with the thought and the principle. He explained why arbitration methods did not meet the need or offer a solution. "Arbitration," he said with prophetic insight, "is not the remedy. Arbitrators are selected after a controversy has arisen, and passions and prejudices are aroused. They represent the two parties, generally with an umpire to hold the balance between them. No fundamental principles are settled by their decision, — only the immediate question is settled, and that usually by a compromise! A Permanent Court exists before the controversy arises; its existence tends to abate the prejudices and passions which that controversy otherwise would kindle. . . . And by its decisions it settles principles that will prevent future disputes of a similar character from arising."

At the time, in the early nineties, all this seemed the picture of a Poet; the fantasy of a Preacher; an old man's dream! But it was a vision, not a dream; and the aged seer was never weary of unfolding it. He came back to it again and again at Mohonk Conferences; and he preached about it so incessantly that the people in his pews grew tired of the subject. He was thirty years, or more, ahead of his time; that was all! He was obeying his own motto to "Look forward, and not back." Had he lived to see his prophecy fulfilled, the Permanent Court established, and the Judges actually elected by the League of Nations, his only possible regret would have been that his own country failed to lead the way, and was not among the other nations which chose the fifteen Judges.

But that was perhaps a mere detail — the outcome of forces which could not have been foreseen! Surely, however, it is most appropriate that the Court should actually have been organized; that the Judges should have been sworn to their duties, and have taken their places on this International Bench, in the centennial year of the Prophet, who saw them there in vision more than thirty years ago.

In the days to come, when an Art Commission

undertakes fittingly to adorn the International Supreme Court-Room in the Peace Palace at the Hague, a prominent place should be set aside for some memorial to Edward Everett Hale. Perhaps there will be a portrait of him, or a bust. Perhaps there will be a fresco on the walls which will show a Preacher, in a black Geneva gown, leaning over a pulpit, and unfolding the vision that was given him of God.

But whether it be outwardly, or only on the unseen walls of time, the memorial of this Twentieth-Century Prophet is certain to endure.

WILLIAM EVERETT

WILLIAM EVERETT

AN outstanding figure in New England life in the latter part of the nineteenth and in the early years of the twentieth century was that of William Everett. Because of his brilliant intellectual qualities on the one hand and his temperamental peculiarities on the other, as much for his accomplished scholarship as for his unregulated manners, he was much wondered at and much discussed. The youngest son of the accomplished Edward Everett and of Charlotte Brooks Everett, who was a daughter of Peter C. Brooks, and a sister of Mrs. Charles Francis Adams, William Everett was the child of both parents. From his father he inherited his phenomenal memory, his scholarly taste, and his rhetorical gifts, and from his mother he derived his nervous and excitable temper. Should we seek, however, to account by way of inheritance for his peculiar manners, — or the lack of them, — it would be necessary to go back to some barbarous or prehistoric ancestor, to whom social graces were unknown.

It may be, however, that prenatal rather than purely inherited influences had most to do with the disorders and riotous contradictions of his nature. Dr. Alexander McKenzie, who was his roommate in college, and who remained his intimate friend for fifty years, could say, so far as inheritance was concerned: "The problem is interesting, but is quite beyond me."

The interest, as well as the general obscurity of the problem, leads me to suggest that a great deal may be laid to the fact that two or three months before the child was born his mother slipped, and fell downstairs, breaking her arm. It was a very bad fracture, and Edward Everett besides noting the fact in his journal, wrote to his friend, Daniel Webster, that the accident had caused grave anxiety and alarm, more especially because of his wife's condition. One wonders whether the pain of the accident, together with the terror of the fall, may not have been enough to leave a permanent mark on the nervous make-up of the child who was born in Watertown, Mass., on October 10, 1839.

Moreover, it is not difficult to believe that the experiences of early years and the general influences that surrounded infancy may have acted to intensify the characteristics of a delicate and nervous child. When the boy was barely eight months old the entire family sailed for Europe. The traveling was difficult, the journey long, the excitement considerable, the inconveniences many, the troubles that one after another presented themselves were not what nowadays would be recommended as advantageous for a nervous and sickly infant in arms. The child learned to walk in Florence, where a year was spent, and there he began to talk Italian and English almost in the same breath. But the sunny shores of Italy soon gave place to the gray and chilly ones of England, and for four years he was to find a home in London, where his father was United States Minister at the Court of St. James. And it is now, in the early forties, that we begin to hear about the boy who was destined to become known and openly spoken of as "the infant phenomenon."

Mr. Everett wrote home from London in the autumn of 1842:

"Willy increases in stature and in attainments. His memory is extraordinary, particularly for long names. In putting together dissected maps, he is without an equal in the family, and knows all the countries in Europe by their size and shape, and all the kings of France, from Pharamond to Louis Philippe, by the cut of their beard. In short, he is as great a prodigy as youngest children of three years old generally are."

A little later on the father's journal contains this entry:

July 13, 1845. "Took Willy to lunch at Lady Zetland's. Colonel Arden also came in. Willy acquitted himself with great success, having recited one or two odes of Horace, a passage in Aristophanes, the names of all the railway stations on the road to Cambridge and from London to Birmingham; stood a very good examination in the counties of England, the geography of Italy and the Mediterranean, and the length of the principal rivers throughout the world."

The most popular form of entertaining in those days was at breakfast, and the United States Minister frequently had at his table Macaulay, Rogers, Sydney Smith, Henry Hallam, and Sir Henry Holland. On these occasions little Willy was frequently brought in, and stood up on the table, where he was encouraged to recite Macaulay's "Lays of Ancient Rome," as if to prove to the famous man that he was not the only person in the world to have a memory that entitled him to be spoken of as "a miracle." If the child is father of the man, it may be that there thus was laid in William Everett an inveterate eagerness to show off, and to win instantaneous applause in public. A characteristic occasion of this kind was when he was asked to speak at a dinner given at the Tavern Club, Boston, in honor of Prince Luigi of Italy. To the amazement of the guests and the delight of the prince he proceeded, in the course of a very happy speech, to recite a long and beautiful selection from Tasso in the original. When complimented on it afterward, he remarked with gusto:

"I have been waiting twenty years for an opportunity to get that off."

A similar thing happened when an Italian warship came into Boston harbor and a public reception was given to the officers and men. Mr. Everett spoke, and quoted at length a passage from Tasso. The wild applause at the surprising feat gave him vast delight, and he confessed afterwards that he had treasured up the passage for long years, hoping that some time just the right occasion for using it would occur. There, again, at three and sixty perhaps, was the child of three in petticoats, perched on his father's breakfast table, and astonishing with his memory the London literati.

There is no need to follow him through the years of childhood and of early youth. He was barely six years old when the family returned from England to Boston, and he began at once the steep climb up the hill of learning. An invalid mother suffering from an obscure nervous malady, and a distinguished father who was busily involved in public affairs of one kind and another, threw him much upon his own resources, and left him to become the permanent victim of impulsive judgments and native irritability. And yet his father was constantly solicitous for the lad, and he gave as one reason for resigning his seat in the United States Senate in 1853, that

Willy needed him at home. His solicitude when the boy entered Harvard College in 1855 throws as much light upon the meticulous anxiety of the father as it does upon the peculiarities of the son. Edward Everett had reason to know about the dangers of life at Harvard, for he had served as president for four long weary years, and had suffered endless agony at the hands of unruly students. The hazing processes in vogue at the time filled him with alarm for his brilliant and excitable young son. He turned to his old friend President Walker to see if something could not be done to suppress the worst abuses before Willy ventured into the troubled waters of the freshman year. And when the president prudently refused to introduce any repressive rules, the father seriously thought of sending the boy to one of the smaller New England colleges. But better judgment prevailed, and the lad was left to take his chances with the rest. As a precautionary measure, however, some classmate, older than himself, was sought for who might serve in a way as a guide and counsellor, as well as buffer against possible attack. Young Alexander McKenzie was hit upon, who was entering Harvard that year at the mature age of twenty-five, and a better choice could hardly have been made. The two undergraduates were to room together, and comfortable quarters were secured for them in Holworthy,

WILLIAM EVERETT

directly beneath the suite that was occupied by Professor Sophocles. The famous Greek teacher had received his appointment at Harvard at the time of Everett's presidency, and largely at the latter's solicitation, so that he had reason to be interested in his benefactor's son. The boy, therefore, was well protected, and supervised with care.

He and McKenzie got along famously, and remained close friends through college days, and all through life. The prophecy of President Walker when the boys reached Cambridge was literally fulfilled. He said to young McKenzie, "You will have no trouble, but your chum may, for he is conceited and green." And so it proved. A classmate wrote of him years afterwards: "As a scholar he was respected, as a man he was disliked because he was thought aggressive and grasping. There was a time when Everett could hardly pass a dormitory without receiving the contents of a water pitcher. At that period he used to dodge across the yard, — the only time, it may be, when he ever made a concession."

The real distinction, however, of William Everett's college career was gained not at Cambridge, America, but at Cambridge, England. Edward Everett, both as a wandering scholar in his youth and as Minister at the Court of St. James when he was at the height of influence and fame, had conceived a very high opinion of English universities. His four years as President of Harvard had left him with a proportionately low opinion of American academic life. To Trinity College, Cambridge, the young Harvard A.B. was accordingly dispatched with a parental blessing in the autumn of 1859. Parental advice went with him, and it followed afterwards at regular intervals and in great abundance. There is something very touching in the way that the precise and courteous father concerned himself with the merest details of the son's ménage. He could, with his many friends in England, secure the entrée of his boy into the homes of the great and famous; but the question was, whether the nervous and erratic youth could be persuaded to play his part with dignity and grace. At a later period in his career, when he had hopes of being called to the pulpit of a church near Boston, and was disappointed, he appealed to his aunt, Mrs. Charles Francis Adams, and asked her if she knew what the reason was. And the aunt, who had not cast in her lot with the Adams family for nothing, replied with bluntness: "Because you have no manners, Willy." The father knew this well, and to his sorrow. He may not have had any undue appreciation of the good manners of the English; but it appeared to him that his son had better proclaim himself at once "a poor young barbarian

WILLIAM EVERETT

from America," needing protection. The following letters, Polonius-like in purpose and in perspicacity, are good examples of the many that went out from the solicitous Summer Street household in Boston to the untidy Trinity College room in England.

Boston 26 Sept. 1859

MY DEAR WILLY, — ... Take Mr. Bates' directions, before leaving London, as to the usual and proper way of supplying yourself with money at Cambridge. Let your expenditure in all things keep the "golden mean" between extravagance and parsimony. Your Uncle Chardon says, "Tell Willy to be prudent." Prudent I would have you assuredly; but let it be the prudence of a well-bred young gentleman. Let your dress always be nice, — rather *soigné* than erring on the other side. You are not quite careful enough about this, owing to your short sight, which always makes it difficult "to see oursel's as others see us."

Boston 3 Oct. 1859

MY DEAR WILLY, — ... Sir Henry[1] says that Cambridge is a place where a newcomer is subjected to great friction. I asked in what way and he did not give me any definite answer, except that peculiarities on the part of strangers had to

[1] Sir Henry Holland, whose wife was a daughter of the famous Sydney Smith.

pass a severe ordeal, which it required a pretty ample supply of good nature to support. I cannot think you will have any trouble on this score. Good nature and freedom from assumption will, in all well-bred circles, prove a passport to kind treatment. Sir Henry describes Lady Affleck as a very pleasing and amiable lady. I suspect you will find her a very efficient friend. Dr. Whewell will introduce you to her; and you will do well to tell her at once, that you are a poor young barbarian from America, and beg her to take you under her protection. She will do more for you — if you show yourself worthy of her kindness — than 20 tutors.

Boston   31 Oct. 1859

DEAR WILLY, — . . . It was particularly agreeable to me, to hear that you had made the acquaintance of Mr. Trevelyan. Sir Henry Holland led me to think he would be a valuable acquaintance for you. I am very glad that Lady Affleck has noticed you kindly; her friendship (from Sir H. Holland's account of her) must be invaluable to you. To descend to smaller matters, you will I doubt not make friends with your bed-maker, and get her to recommend to you a laundress, who will, in washing your linen, etc., do a little mending when necessary. When your woolen clothes need mending you had better send them to a tailor, and do not wear anything after it gets shabby. Keep your things neatly in your drawers. Pardon this minuteness, but there is a living nerve of parental fondness, which runs from my sensorium to every part and parcel of your establishment.

Boston 31 Jan'y 1860

DEAREST WILLY,—It is not my week to write, but as I wish to have the enclosed reach Mr. Trevelyan without delay, and do not feel quite sure of his address, I put it under cover to you. It is an answer to a very kind letter which he wrote to me two days after his uncle's decease, giving me an account of his last hours, and sending me a letter to myself, found unfinished in his uncle's pocket, and speaking most kindly of your visit to him. I feel more grateful than I can express for the thoughtfulness of Mr. Trevelyan in writing to me, and I shall cherish Lord Macaulay's letter as one of my dearest treasures, as you will when I am gone, as it is wholly about you. I am truly thankful that you saw him, though but once, and then when his glorious sun was so near the horizon. And yet though he was very ill when you saw him, "his blood frozen in his veins" he writes me, I should gather from the tone of his letter, that his faculties were wholly unimpaired. . . .

The Mr. Trevelyan in these letters was, of course, Sir George Otto Trevelyan, the famous biographer of Macaulay and the equally famous author of *The American Revolution.* He became an intimate friend of the young American, — the two being fellow students at Trinity, — and the friendship lasted till William Everett's death. Indeed, who knows that the patriotic young American may not have had something to do with developing in the young Trevelyan's mind an interest in the history of the United States that was destined to bear ripe and copious fruit nearly half a century later. At any rate, the following letter, written me by Trevelyan sixty-five years after the events described, and without any solicitation on my part, gives evidence of the somewhat deep impression made by the fiery young patriot from across the seas. I had sent Sir George Trevelyan a copy of my *Life of Edward Everett,* and his letter of acknowledgment contained the following passage:

Wallington, Cambo, Morpeth,
July 7, 1925

. . . Willy Everett always showed at his very best, and by no means at his least characteristic, when speaking of his father; for whom he had a filial, and beautifully compounded, feeling. I remember so well his rebuking me for a couplet in a Cambridge boating song of mine:

So at night, when the wine-cups all mantling are seen,
(Whatever the mantling of wine-cups may mean):

"That," he said, "is not how my father used, seriously and respectfully, old and accepted literary expressions. Take one of his sentences:

"'Sorrow and joy are like the black and white keys on nature's harpsichord.' *He* did not say *piano*," added his son.

"By the way, during the War of 1861-65 William Everett did a very real service to his cause and country by his admirable, well-informed, and courageous speeches in the Cambridge Union Society. To this day I can remember the opening sentence of a speech in which he replied to the leader on the opposite side:

"'The Honourable gentleman appears to be under the impression that all the members of this house, except one, have no common sense, and that that one has no feelings, for throughout his oration he has steadily and deliberately insulted both the one and the other.'"

That, as Trevelyan remarked, "was not the usual mark of an undergraduate debate."

The period was a particularly trying one for an American to be in England. The Civil War broke out while he was there, and it was still raging when he left. The Southern cause was more or less in favor in academic as well as political circles, and taunts were freely flung about when the Southern arms were successful. The situation would have tested the patience and good temper of the most sedate and self-controlled of men, but for one of young Everett's make-up it was singularly hard to bear. A kindred disability was in his case less acutely felt than it would have been by others. Most of his contemporaries and many of his friends were camped on Southern battlefields, fighting for the Union cause. But William Everett, though with all their patriotism, would never have made a soldier. His short sight and poor physique were definite disqualifications. His studies, therefore, were not disturbed by the restless feeling that he ought to be at home and fighting. He had a cause to fight for in England, and he did it well. Others besides Sir George Trevelyan bore testimony in later years to his vigor of thought and independence of action. Such a tense personality could not fail to make itself felt, and happily he was never lacking in self-confidence. He awakened amusement as well as admiration, but a mingling of the two feelings relieved a tension which otherwise might have been acute. The Cambridge undergraduates listened to him when he indulged in a glowing panegyric on Washington; but when in the course of a fiery speech on the Civil War he flung back his overcoat and displayed a tie flaming with the Stars and Stripes, he was greeted with uproarious laughter. But he refused to be suppressed, and he was so quick in debate that he was not one to be trifled with.

Henry Jackson, a contemporary at Cambridge, and later a Fellow of Trinity, drawing upon his recollections, recalled that oratory had been a principal instrument in his education, and that he did not allow it to rust while in Cambridge. "Indeed his neighbors in college sometimes complained of the rehearsals and recitations which disturbed their studies and troubled their repose. At the University his real aptitude for public speaking, developed by constant practice from his earliest years, gave him an easy predominance. His methods were strange to us. He was vehement, sarcastic, denunciatory. The tones and tremors of his voice were all his own. In a word, wherever the Englishman thinks that he could not be rhetorical if he would, and that he would not if he could, and wishes his audience to know that this is so, Everett was frankly rhetorical, and made it plain that he was so consciously and deliberately. In those days, there were occasions when his eloquence was fired by his patriotism. . . .

"He had a liking for startling surprises, which sometimes impressed us, sometimes made us laugh. One Sunday evening, when it was his duty as a B.A. scholar to read the Lesson from the Old Testament, he declaimed the story of Belshazzar's Feast with wonderful effect; probably very few discovered that he had substituted a lesson of his own choosing for one not so dramatic appointed by the Prayer Book."

This fondness for reciting, and not reading, the Scripture Lessons was true of him in later years when he was given a license to preach and appeared in a number of Unitarian pulpits in or near Boston, and elsewhere. After the monotonous, uninteresting, and sing-song fashion in which clergymen so often read, there was something dramatic in Everett's way of reciting passages from the Sermon on the Mount or from one of the parables. I remember hearing him in connection with some Sunday Evening Theatre meetings that were the fashion in Boston in the 1880's or thereabouts. Who it was that preached on this special occasion I cannot in the least remember — perhaps it was Everett himself. But at any rate, I recall the way in which he stepped to the front of the stage and recited the parable of the Prodigal Son. As often happened with him, however, he rather overdid the thing in the emotional parts. His trembling tones when he came to the words, "Father, I have sinned before heaven, and in thy sight, and am no more worthy to be called thy son," made an impression rather painful than otherwise, and I remember still my feelings of discomfort when his voice broke with excess of pathos.

On the whole, the experience at Cambridge,

England, yielded him much more than he had gained at Cambridge on the Charles. Before taking his B.A. degree he won a literary prize, and after publicly declaiming his prize essay he published it, together with another essay that had been given high praise. Thus in England, and at the early age of twenty-three, he made his début on the stage of Letters.

Returning to Boston in 1863, he settled down with his father in the house on Summer Street, and brought a glimmer of sunshine into the lonely, darkened home, where the shadows of the war hung dark and heavy. But William Everett was never known to settle down to anything for any length of time. From this time on he was in a chronic state of trying, or of doing something else. For the moment, however, he was set an interesting task which called for concentrated energy and careful preparation. He was invited to deliver a course of lectures before the Lowell Institute upon the general subject of University Life in England. He entered on the task with enthusiasm and did it well. It was something of a compliment for so young a man to be asked to stand upon the Lowell platform; but he did both himself and his father proud. The lectures were published later under the title of *On the Cam*, and are interesting reading still. They showed the son to have more flexibility than the father, and a fuller play of humor; but except for that, the young man upon the platform was hardly to be mentioned in the same breath with the stately, peerless orator who could hold whole audiences breathless with amazement, and who hypnotized by flawless manner and an exquisitely modulated voice.

Before the lectures were published, Edward Everett fell before a stroke of apoplexy. The brief preface to *On the Cam* contains a touching filial tribute, which was as graceful as it was sincerely heartfelt. It is worth recording:

"As I finish these lines, the last written of this book, a feeling of irresistible sadness comes over me, which no one will reprehend. I went to Cambridge with the counsel, the help, the blessing of one to whom, under heaven, I owe all that makes my life worth living. I passed nearly four years of exile in the light of home thoughts where he was the central sun. I delivered these lectures on my return with his constant encouragement and favor; and now that I make my first start on the path he chose for his own, I can only sigh for the presence which would have excused all errors, doubled all efforts, and supplied all needs, and which is taken from me, from his country, forever."

William Everett was now left without the only guiding and restraining influences in life to which he had ever paid a willing deference. The loss was

WILLIAM EVERETT

irreparable, and the consequences of it soon were seen. Curiously enough he now proceeded to follow the footsteps of his father precisely in those respects where that great man had most displayed his weaknesses and faulty judgment. Edward Everett was consumed by a passion for change, which led him from one task to another, so that he left behind him no great accomplishment. He often expressed regret in later years that his life had gone to waste in a multiplicity of fields. He was successively Minister of Religion, College Professor, Member of Congress, Governor of Massachusetts, diplomat abroad, College President, Secretary of State, United States Senator — and all the time an orator of conspicuous address and power. There was one other career that he regretted that he had not entered in early manhood, and that was the profession of the law. William Everett now proceeded to make the same mistake. He seemed to be ambitious to be everything that his father had been, and to follow as many and as various pursuits. He accomplished the feat, although always in a lesser degree, and in one respect he went him one better. Soon after his father's death he obtained a license to preach from the Boston Association of Unitarian Ministers, and was successively Minister of Religion, Schoolmaster, College Professor, orator, poet, writer of stories, Member of Congress, and — in addition to all this — he used a scanty interval of time to study law, and was admitted to the Bar in 1867, though he never engaged in practice. But above all, — though never to the exclusion of any other interest or claim, — he was an orator. Like his father, he appeared at his best and reached his greatest heights in public speech.

His greatest success, without much doubt, as I have said, was won, as his father's was, upon the platform. And yet the dissimilarity between the two was more marked in this respect than in any other. Never were two conspicuous orators more utterly unlike than Edward Everett and William Everett. Against the stately background of the father's dignity, who scarcely ever moved out of his place upon the platform, and whose gestures were few and studied, flew and fluttered the figure of the nervous son — moving rapidly from one end of the platform to the other, pushing back his spectacles, burying his face in a pile of notes or the pages of some book, sniggering at his own jokes, or all a-tremble with emotion. He once made to me this astounding statement: "You know, I am a greater orator than my father was." That was going rather far; and of course it was not true in any full or comprehending sense. None the less it was undoubtedly a fact that he had certain kindling qualities for producing an instantaneous effect which were lacking in his father.

WILLIAM EVERETT

William Everett was a "live wire." One never came in contact with him, whether in private or in public life, on the platform, in the pulpit or the classroom, without being startled by the sparks and flashes of his wit, his learning, and his genius. His body, which was frail and spare, seemed pathetically insufficient for the force and volume of the current that throbbed and hurried through him. Tingling with excitement, his whole frame quivering with emotion, he would fling his text out from the pulpit, or his challenge from the platform at some political assembly, and from that time on till he had sunk back, spent and partially exhausted, there was no opportunity for drowsiness or wandering attention. People often began by being attracted by his peculiarities and amused by his eccentricities, but they always ended by acknowledging his genius and admiring his talents. He was no ordinary, commonplace person, but a vibrant personality; and, once seen or heard, he was not easily forgotten.

His supreme opportunity for forceful public speech came at the time of the Blaine-Cleveland campaign. He was always independent in thought and action, and this crisis was one that called for brave, untrammelled thought. A Republican in politics until 1884, he voted with the Democrats in the national campaign of that fateful and memorable political year, and ever afterwards he remained a pronounced and persistent Mugwump. Henceforth he was in great demand as a campaign speaker, appearing at numerous rallies, where he never failed to electrify his audience, amusing them at one moment by his raillery and humor, only to startle them the next by his apt historical and literary allusions, and finally thrilling them with his outbursts of patriotism and devotion to high political ideals. When the free-silver craze was at its height, he appeared at a great sound-money rally in Boston, and in condemnation of a conspicuous deserter of the cause quoted with tremendous effect Browning's familiar lines in "The Lost Leader":

Just for a handful of silver he left us,
    Just for a riband to stick in his coat, —
Found the one gift of which fortune bereft us,
    Lost all the others she lets us devote;
They, with the gold to give, doled him out silver,
    So much was theirs who so little allowed:
How all our copper had gone for his service!
    Rags — were they purple, his heart had been proud.

It was at about this time that he made one of his happiest hits of another kind upon the platform. The International Yacht Races for the America Cup aroused an enormous amount of interest in 1885. The British sent over a cutter for the race, and we constructed for defence a centreboard sloop of shallow draught, which won. The superior qual-

WILLIAM EVERETT

ities of what came to be called the "skimming-dish" type of boat were extolled. The victory of the yacht *Puritan* was celebrated at a public meeting in Boston, and the yacht's designer, Edward Burgess, was praised and toasted. William Everett was one of the speakers, and he brought the house down with some lines improvised for the occasion in imitation of a rather vulgar bit of verse which was much in vogue at the time. Everett's lines were as follows:

> The Mersey builds her keels of steel,
> The Clyde her keels of flame,
> Our Burgess builds no keels at all,
> *But he gets there just the same.*

I shall never forget the shout of merriment and applause that overwhelmed the delighted Everett before he could reach the last line of his ditty. The thing had a touch of genius, and yet it also bordered closely on buffoonery.

Everett's greatest success as a public or platform speaker came in connection with his election to Congress in 1893, which opened to him the happiest but pathetically brief period of his career. His father for ten years had represented the Middlesex District in Congress; and in 1890 the son, although living in Quincy, and therefore outside of the district, was put in nomination by the Democrats of a district north of Boston, to contest as a non-resident, on the English principle, the seat of Henry Cabot Lodge. The charge was very naturally made that he had no claim to represent this district since his legal residence was elsewhere. His quick reply to this charge was characteristic, and was to the effect that as one of the chief cities of the district had been named Everett, in honor of his father, his claim was quite as good as that of his opponent, who lived in the summer only at Nahant, "in the smallest corner of it."

He fought a lively campaign; but, as was only to be expected, he was defeated. The hold of Mr. Lodge was a strong one. In 1892 he ran again, once more to see his opponent successful. He had gone on the principle, however, that it was better to have fought and lost, than never to have fought at all, — and suddenly it proved so. In 1893 the Nahant statesman was promoted to the Senate, and a special Congressional Election became necessary. Everett was again put in nomination and ran against William E. Barrett. The fight was hot and close. Everett won by the narrow margin of thirty-four votes out of nearly twenty thousand that were cast. He was elated beyond measure, and went to Washington all tingling with excitement, and full of good resolutions for exemplary behavior. And on the whole his private behavior in Washington left nothing to be desired. He had schooled himself to curb his readiness to sarcasm, and to cultivate good will toward his fellow members. All went well in this respect. He craved indulgence, and he gave it. One of his colleagues, however, was William J. Bryan, and for him he conceived and freely entertained a cordial dislike and an active aversion.

His reputation for scholarship, brilliancy, and wit made his fellow members eager to hear him in the House. But in proportion as they were eager he was very fearful that interruptions, or questions put to him while speaking, might throw him off his guard and upset him. He pleaded, therefore, in his maiden effort, that he might have the indulgence of the House, and that his remarks might be left unchallenged till he had finished. His request was the more readily granted for the reason that in making it he did so half humorously and with a clever *bon mot* which won applause. There was a slang phrase constantly used in those days, "to put in a hole," meaning to place at a disadvantage. Everett asked the indulgence of members, saying that it would be easy by interruption to "*deposit him in a cavity*." The witticism pleased the House, and the expression came to be a byword, — "to deposit in a cavity."

But whether at home or in Washington he could not escape from his inveterate and most malignant and persistent foe. He was his own worst enemy. There is a weird play — by Calderon, I believe — which tells of a man who was thwarted persistently through life by a veiled and mystic presence. When some ambition seemed about to be gratified, when some phase of happiness seemed well within his grasp, when some post of honor or responsibility appeared secure, this strange, intrusive presence came forward, held up a forbidding hand, and the coveted object was removed beyond his grasp. The man became frantic. It seemed to him that he was fated — that some evil genius maliciously pursued him. Finally, when this stranger appeared to be the cause of his friends turning against him, he resolved to endure it no longer. He would unmask this mysterious being, and defy him, even if he lost his life in doing so! But no act of violence was necessary. The stranger, when thus turned upon, stepped quietly forward, removed the heavy hood, or veil, which hid his face, and revealed the features of — the man himself! He had been persistently his own unceasing enemy — defeating his own ambition and his own desires.

That was precisely the case with William Everett. His perversity of temper and disposition displayed itself in a peculiar and yet most characteristic way in Washington. His Congressional position was unusual, and it imposed upon him an unusual obligation. He was a non-resident Representative. He lived outside his district. He was a stranger to most of his constituents, and to many of their interests. The first thing to be done was perhaps to break up his home in Quincy, and move over to Lynn or Saugus. This, of course, was a great deal to expect, and it is no wonder that he did not take the step.

But if he were unwilling to do that, he ought at least to have put himself out to serve in every feasible way, and thus in a true sense to represent the Seventh District. Instead of that, however, he practically refused to have anything to do with his constituents. He declined to soil either hands or conscience with questions of patronage. He was not in the least interested in regard to who would make a good postmaster in Somerville or Chelsea. In short, he would not help anybody to get any kind of office under the Executive, maintaining that the legislative and executive branches of the Government should be wholly distinct. He was entirely consistent and serenely conscientious in the matter; but no one would think of claiming that he was conciliatory. His attitude was good polemics but very poor politics. In fact, his behavior was exactly what might have been anticipated. He made friends in Congress; but he manufactured enemies at home in the district that he was supposed to represent. Altogether, it was not surprising that he was passed over when it came to a renomination. Had he exercised a little more tact and courtesy, however, he might have been spared the humiliation of having a vote of thanks for his congressional services voted down without ceremony at the party convention. But the act did not disturb him. He had given a good account of himself on Capitol Hill and his record there was secure.

Everett, therefore, after his brief two years in Washington returned to Quincy. The death of the friend who had succeeded him as the principal of Adams Academy unexpectedly left the way open for his reappointment, and he was soon engaged again in teaching a handful of unruly boys the rudiments of Greek and Latin. But even this resource was soon denied him. The changes of population in Quincy made the town a poor place for a preparatory school. It came to be a question of either closing the institution, or securing an additional endowment and removing elsewhere. But Everett was not the man to organize a campaign for funds or to construct an appealing programme for removal. He did what he could, and did it generously, — putting his hand deep into his own pocket even at a time when his private fortune became badly reduced by unfortunate investments. When a business friend expostulated with him, and uttered warnings of financial trouble ahead, his reply was characteristic: "Some men keep race-horses; some men keep yachts; some men drink; some gamble; I keep a school."

But the dreaded day arrived at last, and the scholar, poet, politician, member of the Bar, and minister of religion, was left without an occupation and with insufficient money for his needs. He sought opportunities to preach, and his friends got up lecture courses for him. He appeared again at the Lowell Institute, where he had made a brilliant début at the age of twenty-three. What pleased him most, however, was an invitation to give a course of lectures at Cambridge, England. He took for a subject, "English Orators of the Eighteenth Century and Certain English Poets of the Nineteenth Century," and prepared himself with care. Crossing the ocean in the autumn of 1908, he made a beginning on the course, but soon found that in his weakened physical condition he could not possibly endure the damp and cold of the English climate in winter. Broken in health, the victim of deep-seated bronchial trouble, he was obliged to make his way home, almost the only satisfaction of his trip being the opportunity to see old friends, among whom was King Edward VII, whom he had known as an undergraduate at Cambridge and who invited him to breakfast at Buckingham Palace, as will be related later on.

The interrupted lecture course for Cambridge, England, was given at the Lowell Institute in 1909, and he brought it successfully to an end. But it was a painful effort. His health was so badly broken that he read the lectures seated, and only stood at the end to say a brief and touching word of farewell to the Lowell platform. He felt, as indeed it proved, that he had said his final word before the famous Institute.

The last time that I heard him in public, and one of the last occasions on which he spoke, was at the celebration on the part of the Massachusetts Historical Society of the Tercentenary of the birth of John Milton. Dr. Everett gave the oration or address. It was a masterly effort, the more so because his physical condition called for, and indeed necessitated, an exercise of self-restraint which was not usual. He closed the oration with a vision in which he described the young Milton on his continental journey, making his way from one Italian city to another. The orator imagined the genius of each place besetting the youthful poet and urging him to surrender himself to its special temptation. In Venice it is feminine beauty that exercises her allurements; in Genoa the treasures of trade and wealth are laid before him; in Rome the glories of religion. At last in Naples, having resisted all temptations, the Shade of Virgil promises that in recognition of all he has surrendered, "the laurel of the bard shall be his to all Eternity."

It was a truly poetic fancy, and I wrote to him afterwards, thanking him for his words, and calling particular attention to the originality and power of the "vision." In answering, he said that the thing had been before his mind for over thirty years, and added: "I have repeatedly thought of putting it into verse. But I do not manage detail skilfully. I see things in their general aspect, and writing out details is painful, almost impossible." There was the weakness! But it came, in one sense, from excess of power. Pegasus was impatient at being harnessed. He soared in vision, but disliked the sordid work of steady effort. And yet, when all is said, the vision is the thing of value, and the greater credit goes to those who have the eyes to see.

The tales that used to be told of Everett's peculiarities and sudden outbursts of eccentric manners are numerous, and many of them are well remembered still.

On one occasion he was sitting at a public meeting with his hat placed under a chair, where it was in imminent peril of being stepped on. A friend, who was seated near by, being normally well disposed and of a kindly disposition, ventured to suggest that it might be well to put the hat on the window-sill, or in some other place of comparative safety. When the suggestion was first made, it met with no reply; but on its being repeated, the characteristic explosion came: "Mr. ——, I will not be importuned to do something that I do not want to do! You, being a Presbyterian, I would have you understand that I would rather go to Hell my own way, than go to Heaven your way." The hat remained where it was.

If any one ventured to address him as Professor, he would howl with rage. "Don't call me 'Professor,' call me 'Mr.,' call me 'Dr.,' call me 'Billy,' call me anything you please. If you call me 'Professor,' people will think I am one of Charles Eliot's minions out at Harvard."

It was easier to irritate him than it was to smooth him down. If you wanted to see him through his paces of temper, you had but to ask him, during his days as a school-teacher, "How many boys did you send to college this year, Dr. Everett?" That would be enough to cause an outburst: "That's what they all ask, how *many?* The important thing is not numbers, but character: not how many, but how good!"

A Boston minister, on one occasion, was persuaded by a member of his parish to ask Dr. Everett to supply the pulpit for a Sunday. He wrote with care when the time arrived, reminding the Doctor of the engagement, and asking if he would be kind enough to send the "meters" of the hymns which he would wish to use. The answering letter came promptly, with the pertinent inquiry: "You ask for the meters that I expect to use — gas or water, which?"

WILLIAM EVERETT

He was, as I have said, on his good behavior most of the time during his service in Washington. There were, however, one or two serious outbreaks, one of which occurred in connection with a somewhat formal dinner party to which he had been invited. His hostess, having heard of his eccentricities, asked someone how best to avoid embarrassing situations. She was told, among other things, of the guest's vehement dislike of tobacco, and it was suggested that he might be asked to go with the ladies into the drawing-room, instead of remaining with the men after dinner. This was accordingly arranged, much to Everett's delight. He withdrew with the ladies into the drawing-room, and ensconced himself quietly with a book in a corner. The hostess, wishing to be as attentive as possible, went over in due season and joined him, and speaking of his literary attainments, said to him: "Dr. Everett, I have always wondered why you have not written a life of your distinguished father." That was always the most sensitive matter to touch upon, and the outburst was sudden and vehement. "Why don't you write it yourself?" he exclaimed; then took an instant departure from the room, and made his way downstairs, and the astonished lady heard the front door slam behind him.

With care, however, it was possible to keep the sensitive nerves in good condition, and a little display of affection was particularly effective. "Don't address me as 'William,'" he once wrote to my mother, of whom he was very fond. "I am your cousin, and my name is Willy." Another anecdote illustrates the affection in which an older woman could hold him. Dr. Henry P. Walcott, in his own old age, has told me of a talk he had with an aged woman on her deathbed, while he was practising his profession in Cambridge. She seemed troubled and disturbed, and he questioned her at length. "I am not afraid to go," she said; "it's not that. I have faith. But," she added, "when I'm gone, there will be no one left in the world who knows the goodness and worth of Willy Everett."

To people whom he liked, he would write with peculiar frankness. He was to pass Saturday night with us on one occasion, preaching at the seashore in a little local church the next morning, and he sent on ahead suggestions, or directions as to diet, one item of which I recall distinctly. "Don't give me fishballs; I would rather have a sculpin fried in seaweed."

An amusing as well as embarrassing incident relates to an episode at the famous Thursday Evening Club of Boston, where he was a frequent speaker. On this occasion he had consented to speak on Cowper, and was to read, or to recite rather, some of the famous poems. When the

WILLIAM EVERETT

president of the club introduced him, he announced that Mr. Everett would address the club on the poet *Cowper*. There was absolute silence. The chairman of the evening repeated the announcement, thinking that perhaps the absent-minded Doctor had not heard, or possibly had fallen asleep. Still there was no reply, and members began to look in the direction where Everett was sitting. Finally the president appealed to him directly: "Mr. Everett, I thought you had agreed to speak to us on the poet C*ow*per." That brought the irate Doctor to his feet. Trembling with excitement, and pushing back his spectacles, he cried, "Cooper, Cooper, — not C*ow*per, — I never agreed to speak on C*ow*per."

As I call to mind these incidents and others like them, the conviction grows upon me that this formed with him a kind of *wit*. He thought it funny, and he never was averse to showing off, or making a display of superior learning. Moreover, like many people with prejudices, he took pains not to conceal but to express them. He hated smoking, and never willingly lost an opportunity to express his disgust at what he called the "gratuitous filth of tobacco." He had his favorite authors, but he likewise had his disfavorites. Among the latter was Emerson, and all his school. He could write once of a quotation ascribed to Emerson and referred to as fine: "If fine, not

Emerson; if Emerson, not fine." He took occasion once, in connection with some Lincoln celebration, to assure a newspaper editor that Lincoln was not a great man. Indeed, he was vehement as well as voluminous in his reasons for setting down Lincoln as wholly second-rate. His real reason for such judgment was not divulged, but it undoubtedly was a certain jealousy of him, based upon the Gettysburg address which won immortal fame, while Edward Everett's long oration which preceded it passed into oblivion.

Perhaps there never was a man more hopelessly deficient in the sense of fitness. And yet, as often happens, gross rudeness was often due to a desire to be honest and outspoken. A case in point relates to an incident in connection with President Eliot. When Mr. Eliot, as a young man, was first nominated by the Corporation for President of Harvard College, the Board of Overseers withheld their consent. A period of waiting ensued, when no one knew just what would happen. Everett at that time wanted to be appointed to a position in the Latin Department. If, as he hoped, his cousin Edward Everett Hale were elected president, he felt sure of an appointment. It seemed to him wise, however, to have an anchor to windward, and when rumors were heard to the effect that the overseers were likely to yield to the Corporation's wishes, he went to call upon Mr. Eliot. Insisting

WILLIAM EVERETT

upon seeing him, — although Mr. Eliot's wife at the time was desperately ill, — the nervous and excited man exclaimed: "Mr. Eliot, you are not my candidate for president of Harvard; I favor Edward Everett Hale. If, however, you are confirmed — as I hear is likely — I wish to apply now for a position as Tutor in Latin, whenever there is a chance for me."

Nothing could have been more characteristic of Everett; and it may be added nothing either more characteristic of Charles W. Eliot's big and magnanimous nature, that in due season the appointment, which had been asked for in such a curious fashion, was formally made.

Another amusing episode, of a wholly different nature, reveals him in a happier and still more characteristic light. We have seen how a year or two before the end he went back to Cambridge, England, to deliver a course of lectures on English orators and men of letters. During his early years at Trinity he had had a pleasant acquaintanceship with the Prince of Wales, who spent the year of 1861 at Cambridge as an undergraduate. The Prince of 1861 was Edward VII in 1908, and it occurred to William Everett that he would like to renew the acquaintanceship formed as undergraduates. With this end in view Everett visited the American Embassy and asked that the King should be informed of his presence in England,

and of his desire to pay his respects to His Majesty. The Ambassador demurred. It was not the sort of thing that was "done." Everett's assurance that he had been well acquainted with the King in the old days at Cambridge made no impression upon the Embassy! "Very well; I will write myself," was the petulant reply. He did so, and a few days later came a cordial invitation to breakfast at the Palace. Everett was not slow in returning to the Embassy, where he waved the royal invitation with excited glee in the Ambassador's face and said, "You see, — I told you so!"

The breakfast was a huge success. The King was most urbane and Everett on his good behavior. When they had left the table and retired into the library, cigars were passed, Everett naturally declining; but the King took a cigar and lighted it. Almost instantly, however, he turned to his guest and said:

"I quite forgot, Dr. Everett, that tobacco has always been offensive to you"; and he at once tossed his cigar away. Whether the King's memory was stimulated by an expression of disgust upon William Everett's face, or whether he feared an outbreak, cannot definitely be said; but the fact of delicate courtesy remains. Everett's delight was unbounded, and he did not neglect to tell his friends of the incident.

And there it is well to leave him, — at the table

of the King. It was into such company that he was born, and there, so far as scholarship and intellectual attainments were concerned, he properly belonged. He was familiar with the best in literature, and cared most for those classical authors who have never ceased to reign over the elect.

GEORGE HODGES

GEORGE HODGES[1]

GEORGE HODGES was born of New England parents. His father, George Frederick (Handel) Hodges, and his mother, Hannah Elisabeth Ballard, came from Taunton, Massachusetts. Both families were rooted deep in Massachusetts soil.

Soon after their marriage, in 1844, the parents of George Hodges moved to Camden, N. Y., where the Ballards had a "fulling" mill. There two children were born to them, both of whom died in childhood. A few years later, some time between 1853 and 1856, a move was made to Rome, N. Y., and there on October 6, 1856, George was born.

The boy attended the public schools and, later on, the local academy of Rome, finding his way in time to Hamilton College, from which he graduated as Bachelor of Arts in 1877, five years later receiving the Master's degree. He taught school for a year in London, Ontario, after which, having decided to study for the ministry, he attended for a time a theological school in Syracuse, N. Y. — St. Andrew's Divinity School, which had just been

[1] From the Proceedings of the Massachusetts Historical Society, March, 1920.

organized by Bishop Huntington. Twelve months later he made his way to Berkeley Divinity School in Middletown, Conn., where he finished his theological training. Ordination as Deacon came in due course in 1881, and as Priest in 1882. In the autumn of 1881 he was married to Anna Sargent Jennings of Skaneateles, N. Y., and in the same year he became assistant to Reverend Boyd Vincent, the rector of Calvary Church in Pittsburgh, Penn.

His life work had now definitely begun. He was twenty-five years old. Almost at once he began to give evidence of those capacities and qualities, those varied gifts and marked endowments, which speedily made him a power in the Church, and a conspicuous influence in the civic life of Pittsburgh.

In an outward or physical sense, George Hodges had little in his favor. He was destined to become in time a noted figure in the pulpit, and a brilliant success upon the public platform; but what he became was won by application, perseverance, and hard work. He was not dowered with a commanding figure, or helped by a handsome countenance. He was small of stature, rather plain of feature, and with a voice of no particular power or attractiveness.

But almost at once his peculiar and remarkable gifts began to be displayed. There was a virility about him, a freshness of thought and speech, which ministers of religion so frequently lack. He took hold of his tasks with vigor and enthusiasm. He identified himself first of all with the civic life and business interests of Pittsburgh. He was of Ruskin's opinion that in a great industrial centre the sole interest should not be to strengthen steel or to bleach cotton or to mould metal, but to strengthen, shape, and manufacture men and women. "Christianity between Sundays" was the significant title that he gave to a volume of his sermons. His was not a preaching ministry alone: it was a working ministry as well. He was with his people not merely on the first day of the week, but on the other six days also. His service of the Master was continuous.

This went on for a period of eight years. Then, in 1889, Reverend Dr. Vincent was elected Bishop of Southern Ohio and resigned as Rector. Hodges was at once unanimously chosen to fill the vacancy. For four years more his work was carried on in Pittsburgh, growing as the city grew, and widening, deepening all the time in power and effectiveness. These were the days when Social Reform was coming to the front, and when Social Settlements were being organized. The Pittsburgh rector was early in the field. His church became an institutional church: his parish was the city. He was among the first to catch the social vision of religion, and it was a vision to which he was ever afterwards obedient. In other words, he saw that religion ought to be concerned not merely with individual men and women, but with society itself, and the righting of the social order. As he himself expressed it in his pointed, practical, and pungent way: "We have a long tradition of emphasis on the individual virtues. We are only beginning to emerge from the idea that the function of religion is to save men and women one by one, out of the world, and not to save the world. We have addressed ourselves to the task of making good fathers and mothers, good sons and daughters, good wives and husbands, good neighbors, — all of it excellent and necessary, — but we have only in a vague way, as yet, undertaken the task of making good citizens, good councilmen, good mayors, good employers of labor, good directors of corporations, good landlords, governors, and presidents."

In obedience to this vision, he went out and established in Pittsburgh a social settlement on the lines laid down by Toynbee Hall, giving it the name of Kingsley House. The title was significant. There was not a little similarity between Hodges's ministry and that of the famous English churchman and Christian Socialist. He had Kingsley's passionate interest in human life, together with a considerable measure of his instinct for reform.

But George Hodges was not destined to continue long as a parish minister, even though his ministry was as broad as this, and his parish as inclusive. His peculiar gifts and his inspirational power came to be widely recognized. Moreover, it was understood that he had teaching as well as preaching gifts, and academic no less than ministerial equipment. It was not surprising, therefore, that in 1893 the Episcopal Theological School in Cambridge, Massachusetts, reached out and took him. The deanship of the school had been left vacant by the elevation of William Lawrence to the Bishopric of Massachusetts. The position was offered to Dr. Hodges. The Pittsburgh people were very loth to let him go, but in 1894 he moved to Cambridge, which thenceforth was to be his home. The post was an important one, and he was destined to fill it to perfection. He had found his niche. Besides serving as Dean of the school he became Professor of homiletics, liturgics, and pastoral care. It was not as Professor Hodges, however, that he was thereafter to be known, nor as Dr. Hodges, though he was given the D.D. degree as early as 1892 by Western University of Pennsylvania. Almost universally for the rest of his life he was to be known as *Dean* Hodges, and the title was made use of by a constantly increasing number of acquaintances and friends, and by a growing stream of grateful students.

George Hodges was not, therefore, a man of

many posts, nor of continuously changing duties. He served but one parish, he occupied only one academic position. It is not to be inferred from this, however, that his life was in any sense a narrow one, or that his influence and outlook were provincial. The very opposite was the case. Although a teacher, he never ceased to be a preacher, and his duties in a theological school never interfered with his duties as a citizen and a champion of Social Reform. From the first after his settlement in Cambridge he discharged the double function of teaching in the school and ministering to St. John's congregation. Moreover, he was in constant demand as a college preacher. He went on Sundays from Yale to Princeton, from Wellesley to Vassar, Smith, Mt. Holyoke, and Amherst. For several years he was a member of the Harvard Board of Preachers. At odd intervals he was delivering lectures, either in some formal course, like that of the Lowell Institute, or on casual occasions of less importance. Withal he was active in local charity work, toiling early and late on Cambridge boards of civic reform and public welfare. What he wrote of the famous Quaker, William Penn, was true, in a degree, of himself: "He had taken the world for his parish. He considered himself a citizen of the planet, and took an episcopal, pontifical interest in the affairs of men and nations." He was at one and the same time Teacher, Preacher, Reformer, Lecturer, Man of Letters, Man of the World, and Man of God. He was perpetually passing without haste, but likewise without rest, from one duty to another, and from one task to a greater, more absorbing task.

There were three things in the character and career of George Hodges which call for careful emphasis, three qualities which, more than any others, marked him as a man, and made his life conspicuously fruitful. In the first place, no one could come into close contact with him and not recognize the genuine catholicity of his spirit. Almost equally significant was the extraordinary freshness and originality of his thought, which was accompanied by a delicious and spontaneous sense of humor. And finally, he had a capacity for work and a power of achievement which left one filled with increasing wonder.

Some men are liberal on principle, and force themselves to assume a breadth of interest they do not feel; but Dean Hodges was instinctively, joyously, and unfailingly catholic and inclusive in his point of view. He was no narrow partisan, whether in politics or religion: and he knew how to be loyal without coming to be a bigot. He was a devout Episcopalian, who loved his church, and was splendidly devoted to it; but somehow one always thought of him first and foremost as a sincere, large-hearted Christian who sought to follow in the footsteps of the Son of Man. He had friends in all denominations, and enemies in none. Indeed, he almost gave the impression of belonging equally to all. He made an earnest effort to understand the other person's point of view. It was thus that he could write so sympathetically and with an understanding so complete, of William Penn. In the course of his little "Beacon Biography" of the famous Friend he wrote: "There have been many religious persons in high positions who have been so shut in by Church walls that they have been incapable of wider outlook; they have accordingly been narrow, prejudiced, and often impractical people; they have been blind to the elemental social fact of difference; they have hated the thought of toleration. Penn was almost alone among the good men of our era of colonization in being a man of the world, and a man of the other world."

Quite as characteristic, however, as the breadth of Dean Hodges's mind was the extraordinary freshness, spontaneity, and originality of his thought. He was vivid in his manner of speech, quick and apt in illustration, with a positive genius for applying ancient, historic happenings to present-day events and needs. If he spoke about the Good Samaritan, he took you with him all the way from Jerusalem to Jericho, pointed out the dangerous sections of the road, and showed you where ruffians could easily lie concealed. Palestine, when he spoke of it, became a present place, the Dead Sea, a sheet of living water, the Jordan, a real as well as a sacred river.

He had a quaint, colloquial way of introducing and describing familiar Scriptural friends. It was thus in the course of a sermon that he characterized Martha and Mary as "two maiden ladies living in straitened circumstances." More especially, it was this peculiar gift of his that enabled him to write of sacred things so alluringly for children. His *Garden of Eden*, and *When the King Came* are almost without parallel in the way they attract and hold the attention of the child. Dean Hodges understood as few have done so thoroughly and well the true meaning of "the Simplicity that is in Christ." Never were sermons, lectures, and addresses simpler or more direct than his, and it might be added that few have been more searching. He went to the heart of a subject with unerring instinct, and he lighted it up with positive genius. Moreover, he was the happy possessor of a delicate and delicious sense of humor, and this gift in his case came to be a truly saving grace. It kept him from giving offence, and from arousing unfortunate opposition. Except for his humor one can easily believe that this man would have had no easy time as he came in contact with those who lacked his breadth of vision. For he held an advanced position in theological thought. He led opinion and did not merely follow. He went out in advance of his religious communion, and was extremely unconventional along various lines. His experience gave added emphasis to the familiar assertion that it is not so much what one says that gives offence, as the way one says it. There is a world-wide difference between speaking the truth forbiddingly, and speaking it in love — between the cold, or heartless, and the gently humorous expression of unwelcome opinions. His latest book, for instance, was a radical exposition of the primitive and barbarous ethical standards of part of the Old Testament record. He treated the subject with unsparing frankness. One cannot imagine such a book coming from one of his communion without awakening more or less unfriendly censure. But Hodges seldom gave offence. The heretic was concealed behind the humorist. He disarmed criticism by being armed himself with kindness and consideration. He found no joy in hurting people's feelings, and hence it was that he was such a helpful influence.

But it may be that his most conspicuous quality was extraordinary industry. Someone has said of him that he had "a prodigious capacity for toil"; and that is no exaggeration. How he ever accomplished so much, or discovered time for the writing of so many books, and the delivery of so many lectures, and the preparation of so many sermons, to say nothing of the performance of so many prescribed tasks and the doing of so many kindly deeds that were unprescribed, must ever remain a mystery. No one ever heard of his forgetting engagements, or giving up appointments, or pleading in excuse that he had so much to do. He was constantly saying "yes" to a multitude of requests, and always "present or accounted for" when the appointed time arrived. The very titles of his books, and the dates of their publication, tell a tale of constant toil that does not call for comment. Beginning with 1889 when his first book was published, there was hardly a year until the last year of his life that he did not supply readers with at least one volume of interest and value. In 1892 we have *Christianity between Sundays;* in 1894, *The Heresy of Cain;* in 1896, *In This Present World*, and *Faith and Social Service;* and so it goes on, until in 1904 we have *Fountains Abbey, The Human Nature of the Saints, When the King Came,* and *The Cross and Passion.* Two years later we have another armful of volumes, for in 1906 he saw through the press *Three Hundred Years of the Episcopal Church in America, The Administration of an Institutional Church, The Year of Grace,* and *The Happy Family.* And so he went on to the end, unceasingly at work, either publishing sermons, or editing lectures, or writing histories, or preparing biographies. Strachey tells us that "It is as difficult to write a good life as to live one." It would appear, however, that both were easy to this extraordinary man. After publishing in 1914 a *Class-book of Old Testament History*, and a volume on *The Early Church* (Lowell Lectures), he was ready in 1915 with the *Life of Henry Codman Potter*, Seventh Bishop of New York. Then came in 1917 a volume of sermons entitled *Religion in a World at War*, and finally, in 1918, *How to Know the Bible*. It was a remarkable record of twenty-nine books in thirty-one years: and when it is remembered that in addition to writing books he was constantly contributing to magazines and periodicals, the record becomes still more extraordinary.

When a stream of thought was so copious, it was not to be expected that it should be conspicuously original or profound. It was clear, fresh, life-giving, inspirational, and was drawn from many sources. Dean Hodges never set himself up to be a great student. He made no direct contribution to learning or scholarship. He was neither a pedant nor a bookworm, but a prophet and interpreter of life.

He wrote no monumental book either of history or philosophy which future generations will consult in search of information, but he left a large number of books which will probably remain for many years a source of inspiration. He was content to promote life, not learning; and in much the same way his interest was in Religion rather than Theology.

As a matter of fact, however, his reputation for scholarship suffered from the very simplicity of his thought and his clearness of expression. It is difficult to persuade some people that dullness is not a sign of learning, and it is a fallacy which still persists that if a preacher or author is interesting he cannot, therefore, be either accurate or profound. It is true, no doubt, that George Hodges was not primarily or technically a scholar: but he valued scholarship and he was very widely read, with a wealth of knowledge at his quick command.

A life of ceaseless toil and unresting industry, like his, could not go on indefinitely. In 1915 there were indications of a break. He took a year away from academic tasks and went to Southern California. He returned apparently as well as ever. But the injury to health was permanent. His heart had given way. Nevertheless there were four more years of continued energy and usefulness. In the spring of 1919, however, there came collapse. He was moved in May to his summer home in Holderness, N. H., and there, on the 27th of the month he quietly passed away. The funeral was held three days later from St. John's Chapel, Cambridge, where he had spoken to so many of life and death and immortality. The services were conducted by his associates in the Faculty of the School. They were in charge of Dr. Drown, who was assisted by Dr. Kellner and Bishop Babcock. At the Dean's definite request the body was cremated, and Dr. Washburn read the committal service in the Crematory Chapel at Mt. Auburn.

It had been a happy, useful, and productive life, not without its burdens and its sorrows, but for the most part bright and joyous, crowned with honors and achievements. His wife died in 1897, leaving him with two children. After a period of loneliness he married, for a second wife, Miss Julia Shelley, of Oswego, N. Y., and three more children came to him. He was happy in his home; he had a host of friends and a multitude of warm admirers. Young men gathered around him in increasing numbers as his years increased. He never grew perceptibly old. He was permitted to round out a quarter of a century of service at the Episcopal Theological School, and the joyous anniversary was celebrated fitly. He loved his fellowmen, and love was given to him in return. He served, and he knew the joy of service. In a sermon called "The Credentials of Christianity," it was characteristic of him to assert that "The

Credentials of Christianity are not creeds, but deeds." He could say: "Wherever the Christian religion has ceased to be helpful, men have ceased to believe in it; and rightly, because then it has ceased to be Christian." No words could better, or more fitly and fully, express the spirit of his life, and the essence of his Gospel. Both were a blessing to the world and an impetus to higher living.

CROMWELL'S HEAD

CROMWELL'S HEAD

A FEW years ago, during a summer holiday in England, I was asked to pay a week-end visit in Sevenoaks, Kent. The cordial invitation called attention to the many things of interest in which the neighborhood abounded. There was Hever Castle near at hand, which was the early home of Anne Boleyn, recently purchased by Mr. Astor and extensively restored. There was Knole Park also, with an historic house and pictures, the possession of Lord Sackville-West, "one of the noblest baronial places in all England, almost unchanged since the times of James I." Not far away was the best example of a moated manor house that could anywhere be seen. Last of all, it was suggested that perhaps I would like to have a look at *"Cromwell's Head."*

I confess that of all the sights that were suggested the one that caught my fancy and aroused my interest was the last. But which Cromwell, I wondered, as I read the letter. The great Oliver, the only one of real historical significance, had died a natural death, as I recalled, in 1658, and had been buried with majestic pomp in England's famous Abbey. Richard, his son, so far as I remembered, had died in strict retirement after his own short reign and the restoration of the Stuarts. Then there was Thomas Cromwell, the ecclesiastical reformer under Henry VIII, who wrought such ruin among English monasteries and destroyed so much in the way of architectural beauty and real value. This Cromwell, failing to accept the wise advice of Wolsey, and not having "flung away ambition," came beneath the full displeasure of his master. He was cast into the Tower and laid his head upon the block. It occurred to me, therefore, that the head in question was the head of Thomas Cromwell, the enemy of England's papal grandeur.

In this, however, I was mistaken. The interesting relic that I went to see, and which, it may be, is somewhere on exhibition still, was said to be the actual head of Oliver Cromwell — the great Protector and Puritan reformer, whose glorious but stormy life came to an end in 1658. How the head became preserved; how it happened to be severed from the body, and whether, indeed, it be the actual head (regarding which I have but little doubt myself), are questions which involve a weird and somewhat tragic chapter in the great romance of history. The fate of great men in their life often becomes repeated in their death, and the rage and fury which, living, they can hold at bay, descend at times without restraint upon

CROMWELL'S HEAD

their memories, if not indeed upon their persons. So, at least, it was with the mighty Cromwell.

Oliver Cromwell died, as I have said, in 1658, on the anniversary of his greatest victories, at Worcester and Dunbar. As he lay upon his deathbed, a storm so fierce and furious roared without that the roofs were torn from London houses, and the largest trees were levelled to the ground. It seemed as if all Nature were upheaved, and as if a world-convulsion were drawing near. The dying man appears to have suffered from some form of fever and ague — a kind of Tertian Ague, Carlyle says, and adds, a "bastard tertian, the old doctors called it." The hand of death was on him for some weeks before the end. George Fox, the Quaker, met him riding in Hampton Park and wrote: "Before I came to him, as he rode at the head of the Life Guards, I saw and felt a waft of death go forth against him, and when I came to him he looked like a dead man." Yet his vigor held out to the last, and he felt assured he would recover. "Do not think I shall die," he burst out with feverish energy to the physicians gathered around him; "say not I have lost my reason. I tell you the truth; I know it from better authority than any of you can have from Galen or Hippocrates; it is the answer of God, Himself, to our prayers."

Nevertheless, the prayers were answered otherwise than he anticipated, and he passed away on Friday, September 3d. The records have it that the next day, in the presence of the physicians, the body was embalmed. "This afternoon," says the *Public Intelligencer* for September 4, 1658, "the physicians and surgeons appointed by order of the council to embowel and embalm the body of his Late Highness, and fill the same with sweet odors, performed their duty."

Almost immediately after this, however, rumor began her work, and the most contradictory, as well as unlikely, stories came to be told. "The legends," says Frederic Harrison, "which have gathered round the remains of Oliver are almost as strange as those which are told of Alexander, Charlemagne, or Barbarossa." It is an indication of the disturbed and excited state of the public mind that speculation came to be so rife, and imaginings so many. Before I deal with these, however, let me state what probably occurred, and has always been accepted as the fact. After that we may look for a moment at the strange and conflicting tales that sprang to life.

It has generally been stated, and believed, that Cromwell was buried in Westminster Abbey. Some six weeks' time was needed for the making of elaborate arrangements. A majestic state-funeral was then held, with much display of civic and military rites, the cost of which was enormous.

CROMWELL'S HEAD

No expense was spared. The sum of £60,000 was voted; but it proved too little. The gorgeous ceremony is said to have been "exactly imitated" from the funeral of Philip II of Spain, "who had died on the same day sixty years before." In Evelyn's famous diary occur these words, under date of Nov. 22, 1658:

"Saw the superb funerall of the Protector. He was carried from Somerset House in a velvet bed of state drawn by six horses, houss'd with the same; the pall held up by his new Lords; Oliver lying in effigie in royal robes, and crown'd with a crown, sceptre, and globe like a king; the pendants and guidons were carried by the officers of the army; and the imperial banners, achievements, &c. by the heraulds in their coates; a rich caparison'd horse, embroider'd all over with gold; a knight of honour arm'd cap-a-pie; and, after all, his guards, souldiers, and innumerable mourners. In this equipage they proceeded to Westminster; but it was the joyfullest funerall I ever saw, for there were none that cried but dogs, which the soldiers hooted away with a barbarous noise, drinking and taking tobacco in the streets as they went."

Thus history declares — but let us look now at the legends.

In the first place, we are assured that the funeral and burial were mere empty forms — that an effigy alone was laid away in the Abbey vaults. The *actual* body, one writer solemnly asserts, was carried off in the tempest by the Prince of Darkness. According to some, however, it was wrapped in a winding sheet of lead, and sunk in the deepest part of the Thames, two of his near relatives undertaking to perform the task. There are those who have gone so far as to point out the place itself as just below Greenwich.

It was commonly believed, or at least declared soon after the Restoration, that the body was taken to Windsor and put into King Charles's coffin, while that of the murdered King was substituted for Cromwell's. This was done, men said, because it was foreseen that if a reaction set in after his death his body would be dug up and insulted. This theory, however, became in time refuted, for the body of the unfortunate Charles was exhumed and identified in 1813.

Again, it was said that the body of the great Protector was carried quietly to Newburgh Hall, in Yorkshire. There, indeed, in a portion of the wall, may still be seen a place called Cromwell's vault. Newburgh was the family seat of the Fauconbergs, Cromwell's daughter Mary having married Thomas, Viscount Fauconberg.

A more common belief, however, and a much more natural supposition, is that the trunk alone, after the removal of the head,—of which I shall

CROMWELL'S HEAD

speak later,—was secured by his daughter Mary and secreted in the place described.

Others believed that the body was carried, under cover of night, to a little town near Huntingdon, the village of his birth. Others, still, insisted that he was buried by his own explicit orders on the field of Naseby. Some one came forward, years after the Restoration, to state, under oath, that he knew the body to have been taken in a hearse to Naseby field. In the middle of the field a grave was dug some nine feet deep, in which the coffin being put, the soil was immediately thrown back and the green sod laid flat. Soon afterwards care was taken that the ground should be ploughed, and it was sown with corn.

All these stories, however, assume an amount of foresight and fear on the part of Cromwell, or his family, which are hardly likely — foresight of the restoration of the Stuarts, and fear in regard to the treatment which his body might receive. We can hardly think that a man so troubled by affairs of State as he was would give such serious thought to the earthly things that might come after death. He had other matters more important to attend to than what became of his body, and without his special orders a secret burial would hardly have been undertaken.

These stories rather indicate the bitterness of party feeling at the time. Cromwell's friends and followers apparently endeavored to deny that the Royalists were successful in the insults that they heaped upon him after death. The insults could not be denied; but it could be claimed that the actual body never had been found. Let us look, then, at the facts as History relates them, regarding which there cannot be much doubt.

Cromwell was actually buried in Westminster Abbey, in Henry VII's Chapel, side by side with England's mighty Kings. The Restoration did not leave him long in peace, however. When the Royalists came back into power it was thought an outrage that his body should remain there. Accordingly in 1660, on December 8th, about two years after his death, a vote was passed by the House of Commons directing that the bodies of the three Regicides who were buried in the Abbey — Cromwell, Ireton, and Bradshaw — should be exhumed, and hung on the common gallows at Tyburn. This was done. On the 26th of January, the anniversary of the execution of Charles I, the Abbey vaults were opened. The three bodies were taken out, and a few days later were drawn on a sledge, or sledges, to Tyburn, followed by the outcries and curses of the people, who only two years previously had thronged the streets in silent crowds when the burial was held. At Tyburn the bodies were dragged from their coffins, and hung upon the "angles of the triple tree."

CROMWELL'S HEAD

In this connection it is interesting to recall that Tyburn tree was near the present junction of Oxford Street and Park Lane. Park Lane in the old days was Tyburn Lane. Thus, where fashion at the present time abounds was once the spot where criminals and malefactors met their ends.

However that may be, the bodies of Cromwell and the others were taken down at sunset, the heads cut off, and the trunks buried in a hole beneath the tree. Mrs. Pepys, according to her husband's diary for January 30, 1661, was a witness at this shameful spectacle. "To my Lady Batten's where my wife and she are lately come back from being abroad, and seeing of Cromwell, Ireton and Bradshaw hanged and buried at Tyburn." Under the same date we have the testimony of John Evelyn, Esq., as follows: "This day, (O, stupendous and inscrutable judgments of God) were the carcasses of those arch rebells Cromwell, Bradshaw the Judge who condemned his Majestie, and Ireton, sonn-in-law to the Usurper, dragged out of their superb tombs in Westminster among the Kings, to Tyburne, and hang'd on the gallows there from 9 in the morning till 6 at night, and then buried under that fatal and ignominious monument in a deepe pitt: thousands of people who had seene them in their pride being spectators." And then the joyous Royalist adds, "Look back at Nov. 22, 1658, and be astonished! and feare God and honour the King, but meddle not with them who are given to change."

But though the bodies had been thus disposed of, there remained the heads. These were set on poles and taken to Westminster, where they were exposed in a grim and ghastly row over one of the gates upon the roof. "Went into the Hall," wrote Pepys in his diary for February 5, 1661, "and there saw my Lord Treasurer; and also saw the heads of Cromwell, Bradshaw, and Ireton, set up upon the further end of the Hall."

There the head remained for many years. But at the end of the reign of James II, on a stormy night of wind and rain, it was blown down. It fell at the feet of one of the sentinels on duty, who picked it up, we are told, hid it under his cloak, and carried it home. Afraid, however, of being discovered in his theft, — an inquiry having been started by the government, — the soldier thrust it up the chimney in his house, and there it was left until his death, when it was taken down and sold to a family by the name of Russell. In 1787 it came into the possession of a Mr. Cox, the proprietor of a museum, who exhibited it. He, in turn, sold it to another firm for £230, and this firm had it on exhibition in a museum on Bond Street. Finally, it was sold to Mr. Wilkinson, M.P. for Lambeth, and in the Wilkinson family it has since remained, carefully and reverently guarded.

CROMWELL'S HEAD

It was on a beautiful September day that I was driven through the shaded lanes and across the rolling hills of Kent, to be shown, by special favor, the interesting relic. Mr. Wilkinson, the owner of the head, made a good deal of a ceremony in displaying his possession. A large table was brought into the middle of the drawing-room, with a cabinet, or case, upon it, covered with a heavy cloth. The host began by telling us the history of the head, giving the facts as I have just related them, only in much more detail, and enlarging on the certainty of the genuine nature of the relic. After this lecture, or address, the cloth was reverently laid aside and the case was opened.

I had supposed that I should simply see the head behind a covering of glass. But not at all; you were privileged to take it up, turn it round, and bear it to the light and examine it with care. The sensations, you may be sure, were varied and most curious as you held it in your hand.

The head was smaller than I fancied Cromwell's would have been, to hold such force of will and power of a grim and stern determination as were his. As you gazed at it, — holding it by the broken shaft of the pike, — you felt confident, however, that the relic was distinctly genuine.

In the first place, it had been *impaled*, as history declares to have been the fact, and as Pepys declared that he had seen it on the roof of Westminster Hall. The weapon driven upwards through the neck had pierced the roof of the skull and come out, with its long and rusty point and barb, half a foot or more upon the other side. I noticed first of all a curious cut or rim around the crown or summit of the head. This, I was told, gave added proof of the relic being genuine. For, in the process of embalming, the skull was opened and the brain removed. Only to a personage of some importance would this have happened, for embalming was not often practised at the time. These two facts, which none could ever doubt, — of the head upon the spear and the opening for the sake of preservation, — were important elements of proof. Although it had stood through many a winter's storm, and had felt the heat of many a summer's sun while it remained in ghastly warning on the roof of Westminster, there were traces still — patches, even — of sandy or reddish hair. The lips, too, and the chin, retained thin spears of beard. The nose was crushed, as if the head, in falling from its perch before the feet of the astonished sentinel, had come face downwards.

The whole was not at all like an ordinary skull, for it had a covering of skin which was hardened to a kind of parchment. The state of general preservation was doubtless largely due to the fact that the head had been thickly smeared with pitch

CROMWELL'S HEAD 285

when first exposed to public view. I was sure, as I examined it with care, that I detected traces on the forehead of the famous wart, which Cromwell, when sitting for his portrait, had called to the attention of the artist Lely. "Paint me as I am, wart and all," he had directed with characteristic honesty and bluntness, threatening, indeed, that the work would not be paid for unless he were obeyed.

I have spoken of the head as smaller than I fancied would have been the case. It is on record, however, that so great an authority as Flaxman once examined it, and after careful study pronounced it unquestionably genuine. The famous sculptor was well informed in regard to Cromwell's physiognomy, and was frankly sceptical at first. "You will not mind my expressing any disappointment I may feel on seeing it," he had said beforehand. But the doubts and fears, we are told, soon disappeared. The things which tended, I believe, besides the general measurements, to convince him, were the low broad forehead, the high cheek-bones, and a peculiarity of the lower jaw-bone, which, instead of being "somewhat curved, was particularly short and straight."

I was curious to ask my host if Carlyle had ever seen it. "No," said Mr. Wilkinson, "his attention was called to it when he was writing Cromwell's life and editing his letters. But he answered that he was too busy to go down into Kent, or anywhere else, to see the mummied brains of any man. It might be sent to him, if the owner wished, but otherwise it would remain unseen."

Unlike the great Carlyle, however, who felt himself the mountain in this instance, I was glad to see the relic and to gaze upon it with sufficient awe. I felt, indeed, at the time, and am still of the opinion, that the head should be taken by the nation and preserved — perhaps in the British Museum. Better still, the time may finally arrive when the secret vault at Newburgh Hall will be opened. If the body should be found there, hidden in the heavy masonry, — as many think would be the case, — the head might at last be restored to what remains of the crumbling, mutilated trunk.

As I say, however, in gazing at the relic there were many thoughts that crowded in upon one's mind. Holding it in one's hand, it was not to say with Hamlet over Yorick's skull: "Where be your jibes now; your gambols, your songs?" But, "Where be your faith now, your deep convictions, your splendid honesty of purpose, your triumphant and controlling will?" Was it, then, this little circlet of the brain, one thought, which arranged the firing lines at Dunbar and sent the famous Ironsides with crushing weight, and the fury of religious zeal, upon the hostile army of the Scots? Were these the lips that cried out on the field of battle, when the sun arose, and the mist was lifted, and he saw the hostile ranks give way: "Let God arise, and let his enemies be scattered"?

His was, indeed, a varied and great career, with moments of fierce passion, but with periods and passages, as well, of noble impulse and of high achievement, and a splendid and sublime belief in God and in himself. His was a mind of broad and generous toleration in an age of cruel persecutions. Statesman and soldier, he recognized that there were victories in peace as well as war; and he rejoiced in being able to secure them. If he ruled with a heavy hand, it was also with a wise one. If he trod down others in his stern career, it was to lift up England to a height of power and of world-wide influence which she hardly gained again until our own day.

Few men have called forth from so great a poet so fine and beautiful a sonnet as he inspired in the blind and yet far-seeing Milton.

Cromwell, our chief of men, who through a cloud
   Not of war only, but detractions rude,
   Guided by faith and matchless fortitude,
To peace and truth thy glorious way hast plough'd
And on the neck of crowned Fortune proud
   Hast rear'd God's trophies, and his work pursued;
   While Darwen stream, with blood of Scots imbrued,
And Dunbar field resounds thy praises loud,

And Worcester's laureate wreath.   Yet much remains
  To conquer still; Peace hath her victories
  No less renown'd than War: new foes arise
Threatening to bind our souls with secular chains.
  Help us to save free conscience from the paw
  Of hireling wolves, whose gospel is their maw.

A GREAT CHARACTER

A GREAT CHARACTER

NOT long ago, as I was looking through a file of papers that had been put away for safe-keeping, and for possible future use, I turned up one which quickly challenged my attention. It was marked in heavy letters, "Strictly Private." Upon examination I found it to consist of a "circular letter" addressed to President Eliot. It had been carefully prepared and drawn up in recognition of his seventieth birthday. It was addressed, and sent out under cover of secrecy, to every alumnus of the University, with a request for his signature. When the time came for presenting it, the address was found to have received the names of some ten thousand men.

That was in March, 1904. The great man, thus honored, was to bear the burdens of his high office for five years more. He was to live and work for another two and twenty years — dying at the age of ninety-two. In the course of that address, after emphasis had been laid upon many services to college, state, and world, this appraisal occurred: "More precious than your services as educator, or citizen, is your character." Those words may serve us as a text. I can think of none more appropriate and applicable. For not only was President Eliot a great educator, a great administrator, a great citizen, a great reformer, and a great man; but, more than all else and more emphatically than any other thing, he was a great character. He not only had character, but he was character. Nothing else describes him so completely.

Academic predestination was forcibly at work in the case of this man in his youth. He and the college in Cambridge could not help being attracted by each other. For a full century and a half the name of "Eliot" had been included in the list of officers of government and instruction on the roll of Harvard. A somewhat remote forbear, Andrew Eliot, a minister of the New North Church in Boston, was a member of the Corporation for thirteen years. This ministerial Andrew might have been elected president. He was wanted for the post. For his own part, however, he rated religion higher than education, and he did not wish to leave the pulpit. Or was it, perhaps, that he reckoned the discipline and difficulties of a parish less troublesome to handle than the complications of a college. Another and younger Andrew Eliot was college librarian and tutor, and also a member of the Corporation. Then, in the course of descent, came a Samuel Eliot who established, through giving a substantial sum to the college, the Eliot

A GREAT CHARACTER

Professorship of Greek Literature. This man's son, the father of the great president, was Samuel A. Eliot, who, after serving as Mayor of Boston and as a member of Congress, acted as treasurer of the college, without pay, for eleven years. He was a forceful personality, this Samuel A. Eliot, who while treasurer almost felt himself the head of the college, and was disposed to dictate to the president. Two things are particularly worth noting in connection with him. The first is that he began life by fitting himself for the ministry. He was graduated from the Divinity School in 1820. This was not only in accordance with a popular custom of the day, when most educated men turned to the pulpit for the exercise of their talents, but it was strictly in line with family tradition. The Puritan pulpit could boast of many Eliots, the chief among them all being the famous Apostle to the Indians. But President Eliot's father was deflected from the family calling by reason of some weakness of voice, or bronchial difficulty. He was obliged to give up all thought of preaching. This seems a curious trick of fate when it is remembered that one of the most outstanding natural gifts enjoyed by Charles Eliot was a wonderfully rich and resonant voice.

To his famous son, however, the would-be minister bequeathed the pulpit instinct, and President

Eliot from first to last was a very active layman, profoundly interested in religious questions, especially in their bearing upon character and life, and as much at home in the pulpit as on the platform.

But, if President Eliot drew directly from his father the pulpit instinct, he also had impressed upon him in early life, and in marked degree, the unworldly condition of limited financial means, that nearly always goes with the ministry.

Samuel A. Eliot had inherited what was, for his day, a moderate fortune. He added to this fortune, in a very large degree, by a fortunate marriage. The boy Charles was born, therefore, with a golden, or at least a silver spoon in his mouth. He was cradled in ease, and reared in whatever luxury could be secured in those days. As he looked out, in youth, from a stately home on Beacon Hill, it was with every prospect of needing to do nothing for his own support. But in 1857, when he was twenty-three years old, his father's entire property, with that of his mother also, was swept away by reason of the failure of a dry-goods commission firm. The blow seems to have been met with Puritan firmness, and without complaint, by parents and children, of whom there were several.

One is permitted to wonder, however, what — if any — the difference would have been had President Eliot continued to be a rich man's son. Here

A GREAT CHARACTER

is something that no one can possibly say; but it is not unreasonable to believe that this sudden necessity for work which was laid upon him had something to do with his lifelong indifference to riches, and his incessant insistence upon the happiness to be found in toil, and the dignity that goes with thrift. He would probably have agreed — in part at least — with a famous self-made man who declared it his opinion that "the college graduate was not a patch upon the hard-knock graduate."

It is not, however, my thought or my wish to sketch, even in outline, the long life and the significant achievements of this great man, whose greatness found expression along so many lines. I have in mind and wish to emphasize not his career, but his character; not what he did, but what he was; not his outward attainments and distinctions, but the achievements of conscience, self-control, and persevering toil.

If I were asked to indicate what appears to me the controlling characteristic of President Eliot, — the quality, I mean, that made him what he was, and that kept him from efforts to become what he was never meant to be, — I should answer without the slightest hesitation and with entire confidence in the accuracy of the diagnosis. The crowning quality, which was the shaping quality of his life and work, was self-control. No one could come in contact with him — no one could be associated with him, however remotely, in his work — without receiving a distinct impression of his calm dignity and complete possession of himself. He had the quiet manner that is born of strength, and the bearing of repose that can never come from anything but conscious mastery of self. He drove the chariot of life along a crowded, dangerous, and dusty track, where opponents to the causes that he championed were many, and where hostile shouts from a watching world did not add to the safety or the comfort of the course. But this charioteer, amid the shouts, the curses, and the difficulties and many triumphs of the great arena, never gave any evidence of anxiety, fear, or loss of equanimity. There was no leaping of impulses over the traces of wisdom; no breaking of effort into or against the barriers of legitimate restraint; no catastrophe or accident from first to last. He held the reins in both hands, and he held them firmly, with gaze forever fastened upon the goal that lay before. I saw him on more than one occasion that was well- or ill-calculated to try one's nerves or upset one's equilibrium, or to lead to some evidence or expression of nervousness or impatience. But never, to my knowledge, did he ever give the slightest evidence of being perturbed, or at a loss as to what to say or do.

Some one has said that "the secret of mastery

lies in self-mastery," and never was that truth given more complete or graphic illustration than with him. He was a very prince of self-possession, a king by divine right in the realm of self-control.

In his period of old age, when he was persuaded more than once to speak about himself, he quoted with approval Dr. Hale's familiar aphorism,

> Look up and not down,
> Look forward and not back,
> Look out and not in, —
> Lend a Hand.

He laid emphasis especially on the third precept, "Look out and not in." "I have always tried," I heard him say once, "it came very natural to me, but I have tried to practise that." And it was his self-expressed opinion that it kept him from brooding, and from fancying or cherishing the memory of injuries.

I have sometimes wondered, for my own part, whether the conspicuous blemish on his countenance had anything to do with that stately calm of manner and general attitude to life. People who saw him often were so familiar with it that they never gave it a conscious thought. I have had strangers, however, who saw him for the first time, at a public meeting perhaps, say in a shocked sort of way, "I did not know that — why has no one ever told me?" But people were not told because, for the most part, it was hardly thought of.

With himself, however, throughout his early life at least, it must have been entirely different. He could hardly have failed to be always acutely conscious of it. And I have no doubt that it did much to develop that dignified reserve and quiet exercise of self-restraint which made him appear, as he probably was, entirely indifferent to or wholly unconscious of hostile judgment, or bitter and malignant criticism. For it should not be forgotten — what the present generation seems not even to be aware of — that President Eliot was criticized and condemned, at one period of his career, with a freedom and a fierceness that had hardly been exercised against any of his predecessors in high office. Not Increase Mather in his bigotry, or Samuel Langdon with his ultra-patriotism that aroused the opposition of Tory students, or Edward Everett in his efforts to stop drinking and to put down lewd behavior, was ever more bitterly assailed or vindictively attacked than President Eliot. This opposition grew out of his advocacy of the Elective System, and was directed against his confidence in the principle of utter freedom as the best policy in dealing with youth. It was particularly fierce when it came to the weeding out of incompetent or superannuated teachers. I remember a successful business man complaining to me upon one occasion: "They expect me to give my money to the College, and

A GREAT CHARACTER

then they teach there all the things that I most heartily disagree with, like Free Trade, and all the rest." He aroused antagonism with periodic regularity in connection with political campaigns; for in a Republican neighborhood he was always an Independent, and generally voted the Democratic ticket, nor did he ever fail to give expression to his principles.

But the Great President went his way, walking like a god, apparently unconscious of being the target for continuous attack. And happily he lived long enough to have universal praise take the place of blame — so much so that now it is almost forgotten that the sea was not always smooth or the breezes fair during his presidential voyage.

He was quite conscious of this change, and more than once referred to it — not complaining in any way of what had been hard and uninviting, but referring to it almost as he might to some outward transformation, like a "change in the weather."

He said once, at the age of seventy-five: "In the first twenty years of my service here I was generally conscious of speaking to men who, to say the least, did not agree with me. But," he went on to declare, "for the last fifteen years the atmosphere has seemed to grow gradually different, and now I have been overwhelmed with expressions of confidence and affection."

And what a blessed thing it is when one is

privileged to live through a period of storm and stress, and then to enjoy in full degree the delicious sense of coming down from glacial heights into the Italian sunshine of appreciation, approval, and good-will.

But self-control is more than a conspicuous and shining virtue in itself. Its greater distinction lies in the fact that it is the parent of many other virtues that do credit to their ancestry. Both sons and daughters are born of self-control, and they can easily be recognized because of their likeness to their stately parent.

The first such offspring that I shall name is patience, which grew to full estate and exercised enormous influence in the career of President Eliot. We are told that soon after his election to the high office which he held for forty years, some one — an older man — said to him, "I suppose you know what quality you will need most?" "Why yes," was the reply; "you mean energy." "Not at all," was the answer; "your greatest need will be for patience." Whether or not the story is apocryphal, it is a very certain fact that largely, no doubt because of his self-control, this man was able to exert a most unusual degree of patience. He got many things done by reason of the fact that he was strong and willing quietly to wait for them. He bided his time. He did not force the pace, or push things through before the world was ready

A GREAT CHARACTER

to adopt them. Believing, as he did, in the supreme value of education, he appeared to recognize the fact that the public mind, as well as the individual intellect, had to be gradually built up and instructed. He was willing, therefore, to wait until people caught up with him and saw eye to eye in regard to one thing and another. It was as if he saw himself to be out in advance of his generation, — as a pioneer, — and that it was wholly necessary to be patient with the slow movements of mankind. Thus he finally achieved things, while if he had urged them too energetically or had become heated about the matter when the time was not yet ripe, they might never have been put in force.

For instance, it is said upon excellent authority that at his last meeting with the Corporation of the College, in 1909, favorable action was finally taken on a matter that he had advocated forty years before, in 1869.

And this was true in many a direction, and to a most remarkable degree. I took the pains a short time since to read his inaugural address as president, in 1869. I confess that I approached the task without much interest, and I expected an hour of dull reading. To my surprise, however, here was a paper that was fresh and interesting, up to date, and even now in advance of many accepted principles of education. Not only was the style free and flexible, with a certain freshness and charm of illustration that faded out of his later writings; but the address sparkled with aphorisms and epigrams that call for reëmphasis to-day. I give some instances of what I mean.

"The worthy fruit of academic culture is an open mind."

"A mind must work to grow."

"There is no place so safe as a good college during the critical passage from boyhood to manhood."

"In the campaign for character no auxiliaries are to be refused."

"Next to despising the enemy, it is dangerous to reject allies."

"The less a young man thinks about the cultivation of his mind, about his own mental progress, — about himself, in short, — the better."

"No good student need ever stay away from Cambridge, or leave college, simply because he is poor."

"The community does not owe superior education to all children, but only to those who, having the capacity, prove by hard work that they have the necessary perseverance and endurance."

"Thanks to the beneficent mysteries of hereditary transmission, no capital earns such interest as personal culture."

"The poverty of scholars is of inestimable worth to this money-getting nation."

A GREAT CHARACTER

"Luxury and learning are ill bedfellows."

"Inherited wealth is an unmitigated curse when divorced from culture."

"Two kinds of men make good teachers,— young men, and men who never grow old."

"A university cannot be managed like a railroad or a cotton mill."

"Learning is always republican. It has idols, but not masters."

"In the modern world, the intelligence of public opinion is the one condition of social progress."

"In education, the individual traits of different minds have not been sufficiently attended to."

"A university is built, not by a sect, but by a nation."

Those were the academic truths that this young man threw like a series of explosive bombs into the ranks of the rich, the conservative and scholarly who sat before him; and one by one, by dint of patience and steady push, he put them into force. Consider, for instance, how boldly and completely he came to carry out the principle of freedom, which he stated thus, in taking up the reins of office: "A university must be rich, but above all it must be free. The winnowing breeze of freedom must blow through all its chambers."

And blow it did with steady force for forty years — not fitfully, in spiteful and disturbing gusts, but with the steady force of the trade winds, bringing with it the odors, seeds, and spices of luxuriant growth. As you read that careful address of his, pronounced in early manhood at the outset of his career, you realize that there, one by one, the reforms were announced which he worked for steadily, and slowly succeeded in introducing.

It is generally known, of course, that President Eliot proposed at once, when inaugurated, the adoption of the "Elective System in Studies," which will always remain associated with his name. It is not generally known, however, that he hinted also at a possible modification of that system such as is now in force. When President Eliot's successor was inaugurated, he seemed to propose a definite break with the past, and a radical modification of the Elective System, with its free choice of studies. He suggested: "The best type of liberal education aims at producing men who know a little of everything, and something well. . . . The wise policy for them would appear to be that of devoting a considerable portion of their time to some one subject, and taking in addition a number of general courses in wholly unrelated fields." That is the policy now in force, and it was suggested as a departure in 1909.

Forty years before, however, President Eliot himself had said: "With good methods, we may confidently hope to give young men an accurate general knowledge of all the main subjects of

A GREAT CHARACTER

human interest, besides a minute and thorough knowledge of the one subject which each may select as his principal occupation in life. To think this impossible is to despair of mankind; for unless a general acquaintance with many branches of knowledge, good as far as it goes, be attainable by great numbers of men, there can be no such thing as an intelligent public opinion."

But patience was not the only quality born of self-control which found full growth in this man's character. A kindred quality was tolerance, and a magnanimity of attitude and outlook which was quite remarkable. Because he had big ends in view, and was the champion of noble causes, he could not recognize the intrusive right of petty impulses and aims. Perhaps, too, his implicit confidence in freedom, as the policy to be pursued in all things, intensified this attitude. At any rate, he gave evidence of his quality of magnanimity in early life and at a very trying crisis in his career. The fact has often been remarked upon that when Mr. Eliot was suggested and nominated for the Presidency by the Corporation of the College, vigorous opposition suddenly developed in the Board of Overseers. The consent or concurrence of the Overseers was necessary for election. A deadlock ensued. The situation was trying, not to say embarrassing — the more so for the reason that Mr. Eliot was himself, at that time, a member of the Board of Overseers. He had special reason, therefore, to feel hurt; and in many men the natural disposition would have been to put themselves forward, to wear down opposition, and to hold on even if a serious conflict should develop. Not long ago, however, in looking for material bearing on the life of Edward Everett, I came upon a most illuminating letter of Mr. Eliot's written at just this time, and dated April 22, 1869. It was addressed to Dr. George Putnam, a Unitarian minister settled in Roxbury, who was a member — one of the seven members — of the Harvard Corporation. And this is what it said: "My dear Sir, — In the present state of the Presidency question, I am very anxious that the Corporation should not feel in the least embarrassed by considerations of a nature personal to myself. I hope that they will act with a single eye to the interests of the College and of Education in general, paying no attention whatever to any supposed claims or desires of mine."

There stood out the man in all his bigness, at the age of thirty-five. His personal claims, his interest in the matter, were of no account compared with what was best for the college and would best serve the cause of education.

And the same was true of him in kindred ways when it came to those who opposed his policies and sought to counteract his influence. His nature

A GREAT CHARACTER

was too large to take offence at personal slights, and too generous to treasure up the memory of antagonisms or contentions. This attribute has been illustrated in an incident already related in these pages.[1] Here was an occasion when an insulting request made no impression on the magnanimous nature of the man. And that, I have been told, was generally characteristic of him. Opposition to his policies and a frank independence of opinion never endangered a man's chances of promotion in the college.

Perhaps the most interesting public occasion on which I saw President Eliot was when he bestowed the Honorary Degree of LL.D. on Prince Henry of Prussia. That was in 1902, and the Prince was here in the United States on a mission the real significance of which Americans did not appreciate at the time. As the brother of the Kaiser, and an Admiral of the German Navy,— but more especially because of the gift to the college of the Germanic Museum,— the foreign visitor was accorded special honors. He appeared at Sanders Theatre in uniform with many decorations pinned upon his breast, and was a worthy representative of a great and historic ruling house. As usual, however, the dignified and commanding figure of the President in academic robes made the Prince and the members of his staff seem almost

[1] See *ante*, page 249.

insignificant. I shall never forget the shivers that ran down my back when this American scholar, addressing the representatives of the Imperial Majesty of Germany, had the audacity to use these complacent and commanding words. "Our whole people," he said, "have the profoundest sympathy with the unification of Germany. We all believe in a great Union of Federated States, bound together by a common language, by mutual trade, by common currency, courts of justice, and institutions of credit and finance, and inspired by a passionate patriotism. Such," he added, "is the Venerable American Union, such the Young German Empire." As he uttered these almost impudent words, the whole audience held its breath, and seemed to gasp. Yet to-day, the youthful Empire has fallen into decay, to give place to a popular form of government, and the Prince himself has disappeared into obscurity, while the Great Republic of America, made stronger through the years, is now the envy and despair of Europe, and of such monarchies as still abide there.

I should like to speak, if there were time, of another quality — indeed of two more qualities, both born of self-control — which contributed to the greatness of this character. The first was the capacity for hard and constant work, and the second a simplicity or simplification of life and aim that was almost stern. He took a positive

A GREAT CHARACTER

joy in work and counted it as conspicuous among the "durable satisfactions" of life. He not only knew how to go about work, but he knew how to keep at it. "Much of my life," he once remarked, "is what many persons would call drudgery. Within a few days," he said, "I have gone through the entire salary list of the instructors and assistants in the University, and I do it every year." It was largely on this ground that he was such an open and persistent foe of Trade-Unionism. The despotism of "union labor" cut down the hours of work; and to discountenance the capacity to accomplish more than the average individual amount of output was an utter abomination to his mind, and an evidence equally of dishonesty and indolence.

He himself, I believe, attributed not a little of his capacity for hard, continuous, and pleasurable work to the fact that when he took up the burden of his great office he was just laboring under a crushing, personal grief. The bigness of his task was a solace to him in his sorrow, and he found peace of mind in hard and continuous toil.

Moreover, it was probably because of his extraordinary self-control that he was commonly thought of as cold and austere, and devoid of deep emotion. But the mastery, whether of passions or emotions, does not mean that such impulses are absent; it means only that they are disciplined and brought into an ordered realm of culture and restraint.

In this respect, as indeed in the other quality of stately and almost severe simplicity, he was essentially a Puritan. Indeed, this great character was once described as a twentieth-century Puritan. And he was preëminently that — in the simplicity of his tastes and the directness of his aims. There was a kind of austerity in his disregard of luxuries, and in his rigorous adherence to exact statement, and to what we call the truth. He believed in giving clear expression to ideals, standards, and beliefs. When a belief or custom was outgrown, and could serve no further useful end, he believed in letting it go, and taking it out of the educational curriculum or the religious creed. Honesty was supreme, and permitted no division of control. Thus he felt, and often took occasion to say with Emerson, "Whoso would be a man, must be a nonconformist." There was, therefore, — because of the rigor and simplicity of his standards and ideals, — a decided, and one might say an excessive, emphasis on utility. He had a passion for estimating what things were good for, what use they had, and what worth-while ends they served. The useful, rather than the beautiful, appealed to him. The æsthetic side of life was forced into the background, to make room for what had practical utility. In this respect he was again of course a Puritan — and a very self-avowed and pronounced Puritan, at that.

A GREAT CHARACTER

For myself, however, I should rather feel inclined to go much further back into history than technical Puritanism, and to say that he was emphatically Roman and not Greek. The Greek love of grace and beauty and charm, — of perfectly proportioned temple, of lovely statue, of altar or building set in appropriate surroundings, — all this made less appeal to him than what served some practical end or accomplished some useful purpose. Except for his response to the glories of outward Nature, it would seem that the beautiful made slight appeal to him. He did not care for Gothic architecture, and least of all when it was applied in its proper sphere, and used to awaken and express religious feelings. He would rather see God's sunlight pour through plain white windows, to fall upon the bare, cold walls of a simple meeting-house, than have the shadowed mysteries of the great cathedral, with scanty light which took the varied hues from stained-glass saints and so-called angels. In short, when it came to Plato's three ideas of the human reason, he gave full and glorious assent to the first two, but passed lightly over the third. Perhaps, indeed, it was because he worshipped truth and goodness with such unreserved allegiance that beauty, in comparison, exerted an influence so slight. I do not refer to this as something that calls for commendation. Quite the contrary. The quality that was lacking was a great essential. This, however, should be said, that if two of the great ideas are to be developed at the expense of any third, let the two be truth and goodness. These are absolutely indispensable — these lend to human character its essential greatness.

In the technical and historic understanding of the word this man was not a scholar. There was nothing of the bookworm about him. He did not savor of the library. An office desk, not a study table, was suggestive of his daily habit. He was not a wide reader. He had a thorough knowledge and wonderful mastery of his own language, but I am not aware that he spoke any other tongue. He quoted neither Greek nor Latin, and I should doubt if he read with ease either French or German or Italian. In general, neither his wisdom nor his information was drawn from books. He sought out living sources, and his academic position enabled him to draw upon them freely. It used to be said of the German Emperor in his palmy days that he plied his visitors at Court with endless questions, and that when he wanted information upon technical points he sent for scholars and industriously picked their brains. With a somewhat similar instinct President Eliot had the habit of endlessly asking questions. Whether talking with fishermen or farmers on the island of Mt. Desert, or when engaged in foreign travel or in the social intercourse of everyday life,

A GREAT CHARACTER 313

he was eternally bent upon inquiry. He went upon the theory that household servant, as well as famous savant, had useful information of some sort to impart. His practical mind kept him ever on the scent for what was useful.

An amusing anecdote is told of him in this respect in connection with Phillips Brooks. It is said that Reverend Leighton Parks came home one evening after preaching in the Harvard Chapel and found Mr. Brooks waiting for him in his library. The two men sat down before the fire and Mr. Brooks asked about the service. Dr. Parks gave a glowing account of it all — a full church, rows on rows of eager youth, and all apparently much interested. "But best of all," he added, "you should have seen President Eliot standing erect in a front pew and singing with vigor:

> Am I a soldier of the Cross,
> A follower of the Lamb?"

The retort of the great preacher was instantaneous, accompanied by a hearty chuckle, "Asking for information probably." Considering Mr. Eliot's well-known Unitarian opinions, the humor of the suggestion was quite delicious.

And in closing, what shall we say of this man's religion? He often spoke of religion — he never lost an opportunity to proclaim himself a religious man. He believed in religion as a natural and inevitable attitude, or expression, of the human mind and heart. He could speak of prayer as the highest utterance of the human soul. But, a great character himself, he saw in the development of character the great and all-important function and expression of religion. The deepest, highest, most fundamental emotions of life — like awe, and reverence, and the sense of mystery — were servants, and not masters of the soul. They needed guidance, development and control, in order that character might come full circle.

I incline to believe, that if he had been asked to express in a single sentence the sum and substance of his religion, he would have turned to the Old Testament rather than the New to find the expressive and inclusive sentence. And he would have discovered it — I seem once to have heard him — in the familiar words of Micah, "What doth the Lord require of thee, but to do justly, and to love mercy, and to walk humbly with thy God?" He could say in his inaugural address, "The very word education is a standing protest against dogmatic teaching. The worthy fruit of academic culture is an open mind, trained to careful thinking, acquainted in a general way with the accumulated thought of past generations, and penetrated with humility. It is thus that the university of our day serves Christ and the Church."